"*Mission to Millboro* adds a new dimension to the plethora of books on reincarnation and, in more recent years, past-life regression therapy. Few, if any, of the others provide the wealth of incontrovertible evidence which resulted from Marge Rieder's investigation and research to substantiate her findings.

"Having met the members of this unusual real-life drama, I was impressed by their skepticism and integrity. It is a remarkable example of groups reincarnating. Highly recommended reading for everyone interested in this fascinating field."

—Hazel M. Denning, Ph.D.
co-founder and first president of the
Association for Past Life Research and Therapies

"The subject of reincarnation has been a fascinating one throughout the ages. In the last twenty years we have witnessed the growth of the phenomenon of hypnosis-induced regression, i.e., using hypnosis to reach memories of past experiences buried in the subconscious.

"The theory that we have all lived before and that memories of our past lives exist and might be available to us through hypnosis is an intriguing one that has therapeutic and metaphysical potential.

"Ms. Rieder's work is well organized and presented in an absorbing, exciting manner. Apart from being a book that one doesn't want to put down, it should be taken seriously by therapists and people in all walks of life."

—Robin Ely Berman, M.D.
medical director, National Gaucher Foundation

# MISSION TO MILLBORO

# MISSION TO MILLBORO

MARGE RIEDER, Ph.D.

Blue Dolphin Publishing, Inc.
1993

Published by Blue Dolphin Publishing, Inc.
P.O. Box 1920, Nevada City, CA 95959
Orders: 1-800-643-0765

ISBN: 0-931892-59-7

**Library of Congress Cataloging-in-Publication Data**

Rieder, Marge.
    Mission to Millboro / Marge Rieder.
       p.  cm.
    Originally published: Los Angeles : Authors Unlimited, 1991.
    ISBN 0-931892-59-7
    1. Reincarnation—California, Southern—Case Studies.
    2. Millboro (Va.)—History—19th century—Miscellanea.
    3. Millboro (Va.)—Biography—Miscellanea.   I. Title.
    [BF1156.R45R54   1993]
    133.9'01'3—dc20                  93-6003
                                      CIP

Printed in the United States of America by
Blue Dolphin Press, Inc., Grass Valley, California
10   9   8   7   6   5   4   3   2

The truth must dazzle slowly
lest we be blinded by its brilliance!

Emily Dickinson

## LITTLE EAGLE
### by Barbara Roberts

Your eyes have looked upon my face
   a thousand times or more,
And though you think you know me well,
   you have yet to really see me.

So if you could and if you would,
   look once again at me—
Not at my skin, but deep within—
   then tell me who  you see.

# DEDICATION

This book is dedicated to Maureen Gremling Williamson,
whose early, unconscious memories of Becky
were the catalyst that brought forth the entire story.

# ACKNOWLEDGMENTS

Among the many persons who contributed to and assisted in this research I would like to give special thanks to the following: Lynn Farmer for an outstanding job of editing; Mr. Roy A. Spjut, Swedish correspondent at the Church of the Latter-day Saints Genealogical Library in Salt Lake City, Utah; all members of the Ailstock family, who have been most cooperative, particularly Cora Ailstock, who confirmed that in the 1800s a group of Indians did have a village at the "Big Spring," also known as the "Robin's Nest"; the staff in the Archives at West Point Military Academy; Mrs. Suzanne Christoff; Ms. Dorothy Rapp; and especially Mrs. Marie Capps; and finally to my life-long friend, Bill Hampton, for restoring the old photographs of Millboro.

# TABLE OF CONTENTS

Introduction                                          xv

**Chapter One**      **The Beginning**                 1

                     Liz                               1

                     Warm Sun                          6

**Chapter Two**      **Life in Millboro**             13

                     Liz & John                       13

                     Mary                             15

                     Becky                            18

                     Constance & Ava                  27

                     Charley                          36

                     Honey                            46

                     Elizabeth                        52

                     Lila                             59

                     White Bear                       62

**Chapter Three**    **The Plot Thickens**            71

                     Samuel                           71

**Chapter Four**     **Tragedy**                      78

**Chapter Five**    **The Aftermath**    81

Baby Peter    87

Ruthie    95

Sharon    101

The Family Group    104

**Chapter Six**    **The Epidemic**    114

Sarah    114

**Chapter Seven**    **The Indians**    130

**Chapter Eight**    **Going to Millboro**    140

Charley's Mission to Millboro    151

**Chapter Nine**    **Salt Lake City, Utah**    160

**Chapter Ten**    **West Point**    165

**Chapter Eleven**    **Return to Millboro**    176

Afterword    181

# INTRODUCTION

It began with a slice of carrot cake. Maureen Williamson doesn't even particularly like carrot cake, so it was surprising to her that, while at a restaurant with some friends in November of 1986, she ordered carrot cake with her coffee. Several days after that she picked up a tablet and wrote the name: John Daniel Ashford.

Maureen and I had become acquainted through mutual friends, and she was aware of my work with hypnosis. She had originally come to me to help her delve into some areas of her childhood. She came in one day and asked: "Who is John Daniel Ashford? This name has been in my mind lately since you have been hypnotizing me, and I cannot seem to shake it. I need to know who this person is or was." My first inclination was that this John Ashford was probably someone from her forgotten childhood memories so I hypnotized her again and inquired: "Who is John Ashford?" In a firm tone she stated: "He's my husband." Knowing that Maureen's husband's name was not John, my curiosity was aroused, and I asked her if she knew what year it was.

For the past twenty years, particularly the last thirteen that I have lived in Lake Elsinore, California, the study and practice of hypnosis has kept me thoroughly involved. In addition to helping people quit smoking, understand their phobias, retrieve lost or misplaced articles, face and overcome a myriad of other human frailties, I have a fascination for the other side of the coin—the

experimental side of hypnosis. Dealing directly with the unconscious mind can benefit mankind in many ways, as yet undocu-
mented. Again and again, my clients have surprised me and
themselves by opening unexpected avenues of research and exploration. The human mind is not only vast and mysterious but also
totally unpredictable. It is a source of constant amazement what
people in trance will tell an alert, trained hypnotist. This is particularly true in the area of past life work.

Dr. Brian Weiss, a renowned psychiatrist, has found past life
therapy extremely beneficial and rewarding in treating dysfunc-
tional patients. Weiss has thoroughly documented his work in two
well-written books, easily understood by the layman, *Many Lives,
Many Masters* and *Through Time into Healing* (Simon & Schuster).

Aside from therapeutic value, past life exploration is a fascinating study, because one learns firsthand the intricate, personal
emotions and passions that motivated people many years ago.
Sometimes this differs dramatically from impressions imparted in
history books.

I had been working with Maureen on some present time issues
in her life when she came to me with the piece of paper on which
was written, John Daniel Ashford. During previous hypnosis sessions it became obvious that Maureen was a good subject, that is,
she was easily able to enter a hypnotic state. It is a common
misconception, largely brought about by lurid film depictions, that
under hypnosis people somehow lose control of themselves and
become a willing tool of the hypnotist. Nothing could be further
from the truth. People who believe that hypnosis will take their
sense of volition from them are often so surprised to find that this
does not happen that they question whether they have indeed been
hypnotized. As they learn to trust the state, and go deeper into the
hypnotic trance condition, those doubts disappear.

When asked where she was, Maureen said she was in Virginia,
in a town called "Marlboro" and that her name was Rebecca or
Becky. As to the year, she said: "1861 or 31."

One must bear in mind that in this type of past life regression,
which is what this seemed to turn out to be, names and dates are

often confused. Sometimes the names and dates will be inverted or transposed, similar but different. One person in my study gave the town name as Millford, another said Wellborn. Dates are ascertained by historical events, such as the Civil War. Sometimes even this can backfire. When one subject was regressed and instructed to go back in time to the Civil War, she immediately began describing a lifetime during the French Revolution. Now I am careful to instruct, the American Civil War. In order to get a better fix on the time period, Becky was asked what was happening in the country. She said: "There's a war; the South and the North are fighting." That would make the year 1861, right on target.

The first thing that Maureen wanted to do when she came out of the trance was find Marlboro, Virginia, on a map, if indeed there was such a place. She went to the local library and pored over maps of Virginia but could not find Marlboro. There was however a "Millboro," and it fit the description that Becky had given under hypnosis. She had said: "It's about sixty or seventy miles southwest of Herndon. There's hot springs nearby." Maureen had never been to Virginia in her life, and Millboro was a mere dot on the map. Could that be it? When asked about other towns near Marlboro, she had said: "Well, there's Robin's Nest, but that's just what the Indians call it." Robin's Nest did not appear on any maps either.

In a later session Maureen as "Becky" was handed a pen and paper and asked her to write her name and address. Maureen is right-handed so naturally the pen was placed in her right hand, and I was mystified when she switched the pen to her left hand to write the information I had requested. Becky apparently was left-handed. Maureen is right-handed and normally cannot write with her left hand. Becky wrote: Rebeccah Ashford, General Delivery, Millboro, Virginia. "There!" she said, "Marlboro!"

As was later discovered, many people in my study pronounce the town name as Marlboro and adamantly corrected me whenever I said Millboro. Many people in that area of Virginia today still pronounce the name of the town as Marlboro. Becky said that at one time the town was spelled Millborough, but that it was later shortened to Millboro. In the book *Virginia Railroad in the Civil*

*War* (University of North Carolina Press), the town is referred to consistently as Millborough.

During the second regression of Maureen into the life of Becky, a mutual local friend of both Maureen and myself, Barbara Roberts, was observing. Midway through the session Barbara passed me a note that said: "Ask her if I was there." It was with total shock that I heard Maureen answer: "Yes, Barbara was John's mother, my mother-in-law." A little later Barbara requested that I ask Becky if there was a town or place called Green Valley. Maureen was vague regarding Green Valley, but Barbara insisted that Green Valley was the name of the place where she first lived after moving to the Millboro area. It showed up on no maps we could find; however, later, after we received a map of Bath County, Virginia, there, larger than life, was Green Valley about ten or twelve miles north of Millboro.

As these regression sessions with Maureen transpired, she identified several additional local people whom she saw as being back in the same town or surrounding areas in Civil War Virginia. According to Maureen, Joe Nazarowski, Barbara Roberts, Millie Sproule, and a close friend of Maureen's, Nancy, were all with her in Millboro.

Thus began the incredible story that continues to this day in two locations: twentieth-century California and Civil War Virginia. To date I have established approximately thirty-five people in the Lake Elsinore–Los Angeles area as having lived in or near Millboro, Virginia, during the time of the Civil War. All of their lives were intertwined then and some of them still are today. More characters in this amazing time play continue to surface regularly.

Not all have been regressed. Some, for personal, professional, or religious reasons, have declined to take part in my study. Some have volunteered to cooperate, but have requested anonymity. Others, whose names have been suggested, are unaware that they figure in this intriguing story. It should also be noted that some have come forward after hearing of the study, certain that they were a part of it, only to discover under hypnosis that they were simply not there in Millboro. They just could not see it. Those who, when regressed, discovered lives in this little town, saw it very clearly and in total agreement with others in my study. Little details, such as the sulphur smell that hung in the air as a result of the hot springs in the area, the horse corral in the middle of town, and the area known as Robin's Nest, were mentioned again and again by different participants. One young woman, who lives in the Long Beach, California, area and knows no one in the study except her mother, described under hypnosis all the leading characters in Millboro with great accuracy.

Of the entire cast of characters only three had ever been to Virginia, and those three had not been in the vicinity of Millboro. The town is not mentioned in the prominent works on the Civil War and was very difficult to research except through the life experiences of these inhabitants as remembered under hypnosis. That Millboro is not known to history is curious, since it is revealed through these people who lived there that it had a crucially important part to play in that war, although no major battles were actually fought there.

The events and people depicted in *Mission to Millboro* will challenge the reader, but no more so than they challenged the people involved in this study, none of whom had any idea of the story we were about to unfold, piece by piece. Everyone involved found themselves by turns amazed, incredulous, skeptical, fascinated, enthralled, and sometimes frightened as the strands of the story began to weave together.

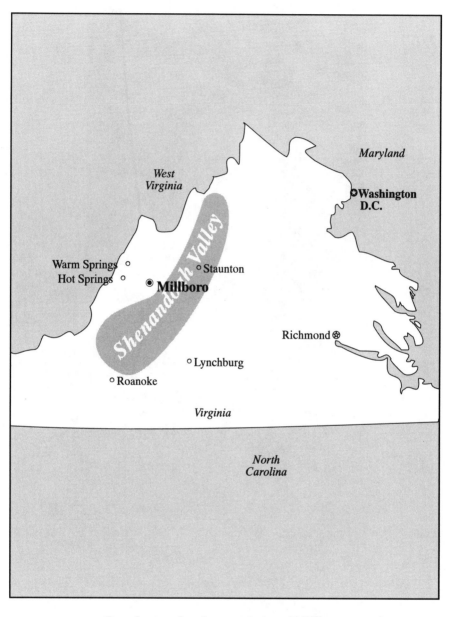

*Rough map showing proximity of Millboro*
*to the Shenandoah Valley*

*"LIZ"*

*Barbara Roberts, born in Danville, IL, 1930.*
*Moved to Michigan after high school. Has four grown children;*
*currently works as a business consultant.*
*Has lived in Elsinore for seven years and*
*had never been to Virginia when this study began.*
*Also referred to as "Singing Bird."*

# CHAPTER ONE

# THE BEGINNING

## LIZ

ANSWERING THE QUESTION: "Who is John Daniel Ashford?" turned out to be much more complicated than anticipated, even after the initial shock of discovering that he was someone who had lived approximately 130 years ago. In fact, although almost no one in Millboro knew it, John Daniel Ashford was not his only name. To his mother and father, his original name was "Pony Boy." He was born in the idyllically beautiful area in the hills above Millboro, known as Robin's Nest.

The story begins around the year 1815 in an Indian village, probably in Louisa County, Virginia, when a baby girl was born to an Indian woman named Winja, or "Raining Eyes." The baby came to be called Liz. She never knew her mother and thinks perhaps her mother died either in childbirth or shortly thereafter. The father of baby Liz was a white man named Frank Gillian. According to Barbara Roberts in trance as Liz: "My father wore a dark suit and travelled by horseback. He was probably a salesman." He loved his little girl dearly, but as he was unable to take care of her himself, she was raised among the Indians for the first few years of her life. When Liz approached school age, her father took her to live with his brother, a farmer in Louisa County, and then he continued his life on the road.

Liz saw very little of her real father, she said: "He lived a long way away. He wrote to me and sent presents. One time he sent me a real pretty scarf, or shawl." Occasionally throughout the years, he would visit her. As she grew older, the visits continued, but in spite of the fact that she eagerly looked forward to his visits, she never had any idea of when they would occur. She would simply look up and see him standing there.

Living alone with her uncle on the farm was a hard life. Her uncle put her to work as soon as she was able, and he never addressed her as anything but "girl." It was a long way to school and she attended sporadically, learning only enough to escape the stigma of illiteracy. Her happiest memories were of the moments when, after a hard day's work in the fields, her uncle would let her swing in the swing on the porch of the house.

Liz recalled bitterly from her trance: "I worked hard for him and he sold me. He got some cows in exchange." She was referring to the fact that at the age of fourteen, her uncle traded her to a man named Jud for a couple of cows, and she found herself married and living on a farm in Green Valley several miles from Millboro.

Liz had become a beautiful girl. She stood tall and straight with long black hair, green eyes, and skin much lighter than her Indian mother had. She was also well built and strong, which was important as she worked all of her early life in the fields.

According to Liz: "Jud's last name 'Aushlick' was Swedish, but succeeding generations thought they were German. I can see a big, blonde Swedish man coming off the boat into America. Swedes as a nationality were not very well accepted then, so he decided to pose as German, which was currently a more popular nationality in the States. Because the accents were similar, he got away with it." It was discovered much later in the story that Jud's real name was Ailstock.

Suggesting that Liz describe her relatives, she declared angrily: "I don't like his brother or his wife. They bought me literally to work the farm!" The entire family treated Liz with coolness and a certain condescension, including her husband.

Jud was much older than Liz, and the marriage came to an abrupt end about a year after they were married. Liz said: "Thank God! I didn't like him and he didn't care about me either. He wanted somebody to do the work. He left on horseback one day, didn't take anything with him and didn't come back." When asked what had happened to him, she said: "I didn't care." Later it came to light that Jud had been thrown from his horse and killed instantly. Liz said: "Jud's family thought his death was my fault. He left and got killed—it was his horse that threw him. I don't know why he left, probably just going into town." Although Liz was Jud's legal heir, none of his estate came to her, as community property laws were unheard of then, at least in that part of rural Virginia. The farm and all of its adjoining property reverted to Jud's family, but Liz remained on the farm after Jud's death because she had no place else to go, and the family, as she said, "wanted me to bring the crop in."

One day Liz was hard at work in the field, harvesting, when a tall, handsome young Indian man came walking down the road and paused to speak to her. She recalled: "He spoke good English. He said 'the Wise One' had taught him. He stopped and helped me work." The Wise One was not a leader or a chief among the local Indians, but he clearly was a figure of importance. The young Indian's name was White Eagle, but the tribe and his family called him Little Eagle, a holdover from his not-too-distant childhood. He was roughly a year or so older than Liz. For the first time in her life, someone offered to share her labor. Little Eagle pitched in and not only helped her with that day's harvest but began showing up on a regular basis to work side by side with her. Before long the two began falling deeply in love. For the first time, the sun began to shine in the bleak existence of this young woman.

When Little Eagle and Liz decided to marry, she gladly deserted the farm where she had been so unhappy, and the two moved to the Indian village high above Millboro called Robin's Nest. It would be hard to imagine a more beautiful spot. The village was situated at the crest of a mountain and tucked into thick groves of slender trees. Liz described it: "Robin's Nest looked out over everything. The village had hills on three sides, and the fourth side looked out over everything in the valley." Pure, sweet air rustled the leaves and bent the grasses of several rich, lush meadows. Areas were cleared for crops and for tepees and wickiups. The Indians who lived in Robin's Nest were from a mixture of tribes that coexisted peacefully in this exquisite spot. Most were taking refuge from the United States government, which was diligently trying to round up and relocate Indians onto reservations. The hunting and fishing in Robin's Nest were excellent and the spot remote. Liz found it close to paradise.

She did not live with Little Eagle until after their marriage. Instead, some of the women in the village built her a small, square structure that Liz called "a wickiup. It was big and covered with hides of some sort, maybe deer hides. I slept on the floor on pallets with skins and furs." She was so happy with her new life that she found herself with a new name; the Indians renamed her "Singing Bird" because she sang for joy throughout the day. Everyone in the village accepted her and treated her well. She recalled: "There was a special area reserved for white women who were involved with Indians, but when I lived in Robin's Nest, I did not stay with them, I lived right in the camp." Part of this was due to the fact that she had Indian blood and part from the fact that Little Eagle was the son of the Wise One.

A number of others in my study mentioned that the Indians in Robin's Nest were very friendly, industrious, and enterprising. Liz said: "The Indians used a lot of gourds. They hollow them out and smashed up corn, which made really hard bread. Later they made a deal with the mill in town to grind the corn for a share of it. The Indians also sold food in town." They made a good deal of money trapping, training, and selling the horses that ran wild in the canyons outside of town. They bartered for and purchased some supplies in town, but for the most part they were quite self-sufficient in their mountain paradise.

The women in the village spent a long time planning the wedding of Singing Bird and Little Eagle. They made a wedding dress for Singing Bird, which was of the very finest hides, off-white and trimmed with fringe and beads. There was also a pair of matching hide boots, trimmed with fringe. A huge bonfire was built and the entire village turned out for the event. Liz said: "There was an instrument played at the ceremony. It was two sticks with wire strung taut between them." Part of the ceremony was a dance Liz performed. The men of the tribe formed a passageway for the bride and groom by standing in two long parallel lines about three feet apart, with their backs to each other. Little Eagle sat at one end of the line and slowly, sensuously, Singing Bird danced toward him from the other end, in an erotic and fluid dance. When she stood before him, he rose, took her hand in his, raised it over his head and proclaimed to the tribe and the universe: "This is my woman!"

When Barbara came out of the hypnotic state after that particular session, she was laughing and said: "I could have seduced any man in the world with that dance! Wonder where I learned it?!"

Sex prior to marriage was taboo in Singing Bird's adopted Indian society. After marriage, in their tribe, the woman introduced the sexual moves by rubbing oil on her husband's body. Singing Bird became pregnant shortly after her marriage, but to her dismay and grief, she quickly lost the baby. In her zeal to be a working member of the tribe she had overdone it and lifted too many heavy baskets of corn, carrots, and grain. Her disappointment soon turned to elation however, as she became pregnant almost immediately afterward and this time bore a healthy son. When the baby boy— who, according to custom, had not yet been named—began to walk, they called him "Pony Boy" because, as Liz claimed: "He had a funny little walk. He pranced like a little pony." The boy had inherited his mother's beautiful green eyes and light skin. His hair was thick and dark like that of both his parents, and he had his father's high, chiselled cheekbones.

The time that Liz spent at Robin's Nest as Singing Bird was the happiest of her entire life. The work was extremely hard, but unlike the drudgery of her earlier years, it was a labor of love. She and Little Eagle were united in a deep and true love, in soul and spirit as well as heart. Liz said: "There was more than just a physical attraction. He was the perfect man, a beautiful person. As he matured, he was the one who made all the decisions for the whole tribe. He became 'the Wise One.'"

## WARM SUN

In the beginning, the hypnosis sessions were conducted on an individual basis, but a short way into my study an idea grew that proved really fruitful. It was discovered that if more than one person were regressed at a time, they would get into it much more easily, would relate to each other and almost forget that an outsider was present. They were less inhibited. My subjects laughed, joked, and squabbled with each other, and much more information came out of these sessions than if only one person were entranced. They seemed to build on what each other was saying. One would remember some detail that would set the other (or others) off, and their collective descriptions and emotions would just come bubbling out. Sometimes the laughter and hilarity were so boisterous that keeping control became a challenge. At other times they would get into such arguments that they would appear ready to come to blows. Emotions were always close to the surface, and it was fascinating to watch. I found that regressing three was even more fruitful than two, and at one time a session was taped in which five subjects were regressed together. Things really moved at a clip during that one! Robin Park heard a lecture regarding these Millboro regressions and called me one day saying that the subject was haunting her. She is a tall, reddish-blonde, part Jewish, Canadian woman, but when regressed she went back to an unusually short Indian woman.

Many first regression sessions are unrewarding and Robin's was no exception. Not much was learned, except that she was a very short Indian woman—about four feet tall. The only thing memorable in Robin's first hypnosis session was that this Indian woman seemed to be either incredibly stupid or was playing dumb. No matter what was asked of her, she answered: "I don't know; you'll have to ask my husband about that."

*"WARM SUN"*

*Robin Park, born in Moose Jaw, Saskatchewan, 1925.*
*Served in Royal Canadian Air Force 1942–46.*
*Married after WWII; mother of two children.*
*Has lived outside of Elsinore for thirty years; had never*
*been to Virginia or heard of Millboro prior to this study.*

Our second session yielded more. On a hunch, Robin was regressed with Barbara Roberts (as Singing Bird), and this proved to be the key that unlocked Robin's reticence. The two women went back to the time prior to the Civil War and decided that Robin's Indian name had been "Warm Sun." They were at the point in time when Singing Bird was fairly new to the tribe and pregnant with Pony Boy. The wedding of Singing Bird and Little Eagle had been a big event in Robin's Nest; the ceremony and the dancing went on for a long time. Singing Bird could see Warm Sun at the ceremony, dancing, and Warm Sun was very much aware of Singing Bird and her beautiful leather wedding dress.

I asked Warm Sun to tell me how the village was laid out. She replied: "The chief has the first dwelling and the Wise One is next.

Singing Bird and Little Eagle had the next dwelling as Little Eagle was a man of high stature in the tribe. My family and I lived way over on the far edge of the village, on the side of a mountain. There is a place where everybody meets, where the ceremonies are held. There are different groups and tribes together here."

Since this was a time when the federal government was actively concentrating their efforts to relocate Indian tribes onto reservations, it is possible that the various segments of tribes at Robin's Nest represented individuals hiding out from the government, banding together for strength.

Warm Sun and Singing Bird knew each other at the village and had a mutually enjoyable relationship somewhere between intimate friendship and casual acquaintances. Warm Sun said: "We would meet in the parley area; we would sit on the ground. Singing Bird taught me English and I taught her the Indian ways."

Warm Sun described her husband and family: "My husband is very tall. I have one baby that comes to my knee and another one on the way. The little ones don't wear much—it doesn't get very cold. My baby wears a long leather vest and cloth that I wrap around his bottom and tie on the sides."

Warm Sun was born and died in Robin's Nest, and she left it seldom. On a couple of very special occasions she was allowed to go into Millboro to the general store with her husband. Warm Sun said: "He didn't buy anything; he just traded things to get some oil or whatever he needed. I stand by the door." Asked if she had ever gone inside, her reply was: "Oh no!" Her going inside was just not done. Each time she would accompany her husband to town, she would stand in the same place, and as her husband opened the door to enter, the door would smack her on the head. It never occurred to her to stand to one side where the door would not hit her in the head. Warm Sun was definitely not very bright! During her few trips into town, Warm Sun was aware of the horse corral. She said: "It's over on the other side of the road. The man there is mean to the horses—he's mean period!" Singing Bird added: "There's too many horses in there; there's not enough room." Warm Sun described the man who trained the horses: "He has dark brown hair and his eyes are light brown. I think he has a little beard. It's not really a beard; he just doesn't take care of himself. He is dirty, scruffy, about thirty years old. He's well built with a big chest, pretty tall and husky. He stands funny, kind of cocky. He wears his hat down over one eye."

Warm Sun and Singing Bird told me of the stills that dotted the hills outside of town, Warm Sun adding: "My husband told me about them; everybody knows about them. The settlers have the stills." Singing Bird said: "I have never seen a still but I know about them." Then Singing Bird pointed and laughed: "That's the trail; they bring the liquor down that trail. The settlers use the liquor to bribe the Indians."

When the Indians went out hunting, they invariably would run into scouts and soldiers from both sides of the war who wanted information. Most of the soldiers would carry flasklike leather containers filled with some sort of liquor, which they would offer to the Indians in exchange for information. Warm Sun: "When the Indian men are hunting, they meet scouts and the scouts offer them 'tea.' It's really home brew and it burns all the way down. It's like lightning, firewater. It's a big joke among the Indians. They'll say to those who had been out hunting, 'Have you been offered any Yankee tea-see?'" Both women giggled at this. Singing Bird said: "The Indians brought the liquor back. I did not approve of this." Singing Bird was strongly against alcohol. The uncle who raised her drank, and he wasn't too bad until he got his jug of liquor; then he became very nasty.

According to Warm Sun, they did a lot of singing in Robin's Nest. She said: "My husband used to sing a lot. Sometimes everybody sang together. I can see my husband singing. He's doing this dance, one, two, three, one, two, three and claps his hands together." Suddenly, she began clapping her hands loudly and moving her feet in a dancing motion, thrashing her body about on the bed, causing Singing Bird on the other side to roll back and forth. Continuing to clap her hands and thrash her feet, she let go of several ear-splitting shrieks and howls, which thoroughly startled the hypnotist. She explained: "He's preparing himself for the hunt—he has to get himself psyched out." Then she made a long hissing sound and said: "He's trying to be an owl because the owl goes down and gets the mouse." After a few more seconds of thrashing and howling like an owl, unexpectedly she started to cry. Finally she said: "He's going hunting and I never know if he's going to come back. I love him so much." After Warm Sun had regained her composure and stopped crying, Singing Bird declared rather smugly: "Little Eagle works with the Wise One; he doesn't have to go out hunting."

Later in the conscious state, Warm Sun explained: "My husband would do a hooting owl song patterned after the owls before they swoop down and pounce on a mouse. He was noted as a good hunter. He was fearless, but I knew that under it all he was really scared. He would do the hooting owl thing to get in the proper mood. By doing the owl dance he would try to acquire the visual acuity of the owl. It depended on what they were going to hunt. If they were going to hunt deer, they would do a different dance. They actually tried to put themselves in the mind of the animal." Singing Bird added: "If they weren't scared before they went on the hunt, then they weren't showing any courage. By the time they left on the hunt, they were in a very macho frame of mind."

Hunting for the tribe was a more dangerous occupation than we today might realize. About a year after this session, Robin brought her former husband, Don, to see me, declaring that he had been Warm Sun's husband back in Robin's Nest. Don agreed to participate in the research.

Placed into a deep trance, he was instructed to regress back to the era of the American Civil War. Suddenly his body began to twitch and jerk, his eyes flew open, and in a panic he screamed: "I'm being eaten by a bear." After regaining his composure and coming out of the trance, he explained that he was hunting and had come across two small bear cubs. While he was pondering how to get them back to the Indian village, the mother appeared and attacked him, killing him with her claws and teeth.

Despite the fact that Don really wanted to continue being regressed into that lifetime, his unconscious mind raised an impenetrable barrier, and the project with him was abandoned. For many years before they were forced out of Robin's Nest, the Indians had an increasingly difficult time. The settlers were moving in in larger numbers, gobbling up the land that the Indians used for hunting, and the tribe became more restricted in the hunting grounds available to them. There began to be conflicts between the Indians and settlers that had never existed before. If the Indians found a chicken that belonged to a white settler and they were hungry, they would simply take it. The Indians, according to Singing Bird and Warm Sun, did not realize that any one person or group of persons "owned" any food. If it was there lying about, it was fair game for anyone who was hungry. The Robin's Nest Indians as a whole were very peaceful people and could not understand fighting of any kind. They could not comprehend why the white man felt compelled to bully them, nor why the white brothers were intent on killing each other.

Warm Sun had married very young, before she was even fully grown. She loved her husband and children very much, but unfortunately died from a fever before reaching middle age. She was aware that she was dying and was able to accept it, but was desolate at the thought of being unable to see her children grow up. Her husband, out hunting, was told when he returned home that his wife was dying of the fever. Coming into the tepee to talk to her, he bade her to go in peace and assured her that the children would be raised as she would have wanted them to be. In part he was referring to their diet. Meat was the main staple of the diet in the village, and there was always a pervasive rank smell in the air from the many skins hanging about in various stages of drying. Warm Sun's grandmother, however, had steered her toward a diet of berries and vegetables, and her husband reassured her that he would continue to see that their children ate the way she had taught them.

When talking with Robin about the first regressions, she stated that in this life it has been an overriding goal of hers to live long enough to raise her family, which she has successfully done, and her experience of Warm Sun illuminated that somewhat irrational fear. Robin also said that she, as Warm Sun, was deliberately reticent because Warm Sun did not like white people, and the hypnotist was "one of them" and not to be trusted. Both Warm Sun and Singing Bird considered the Indians to be their family and were very protective of them. Barbara too admitted that the first time she was regressed she withheld a lot of information, thinking: "It's none of her business!" Eventually the fear of being exploited diminished, and they both felt able to speak freely.

CHAPTER TWO

# LIFE IN MILLBORO

*"If heaven is as beautiful as Millboro
how glorious eternity will be!"*　　Becky

## LIZ & JOHN

SINGING BIRD'S LOVE OVERFLOWED onto the whole tribe and they returned it in full. So it was heartbreaking when Pony Boy was about two years old that the Indian council decided that she should take the baby and move into town—to Millboro. Almost no one outside the Indian settlement knew about her liaison with Little Eagle; her real father and a few other close and trusted friends were the only ones who knew where she was. It was agreed by the council that the child would use the "Aushlick" name since that was Liz's widowed name. Liz was directed to give the baby a Christian name, preferably one that had been established in the Aushlick family. She chose "Andrew" after an illustrious forebear, but she always called the child "John" because she thought that name denoted strength. The idea behind the council's decision was, Liz said: "They wanted John to get an education and bring it back to help our tribe." No one would question the appearance of Liz and her Christian-named child in the white community of Millboro, and John would therefore get an education in the white man's school.

*13*

Liz explained: "The only school for the Indians was held by the Wise One when he had time to teach them. The Wise One taught his son, Little Eagle, to speak English. I used a lot of sign language with the Indian women."

While Liz was filled with anguish at the thought that she must leave Robin's Nest and return to the white man's world, in her heart she knew it was the proper decision, especially for her son. If she remained much longer in the village, eventually the world would know who John's real father was and the boy would lose all chance of an education. If she left while he was still young, she could pass him off as an Aushlick. There was just enough European blood in him that it modified any Indian appearance, and of course there were those striking green eyes. This was extremely important, because if the truth had ever surfaced, the child would not only have been banished from school, but he and his mother from the town itself, and made to return to the Indian settlement.

Little Eagle used some sort of government script to buy a house in town for Liz and John. She described the house: "It was narrow and long, way up off the ground. It was frameworklike underneath. There wasn't any skirt around the bottom, just latticelike work." Little Eagle and Liz had to proceed very cautiously once she moved into Millboro. Liz said: "We had to live separate because our marriage would not have been accepted in the white community. His people accepted me, but the white people never would have accepted him." If the community had suspected that she was involved with an Indian, and even worse, that he was the father of her child, both she and her son would have been completely ostracized. She said: "He used to come and visit me at the house. I used to see him out in the back. John never saw him. He used to wait in the woods out back until he was sure that nobody was there and that John was asleep, then he would come and tap on the back door." In the morning he would leave just before sunrise. This arrangement went on until Liz died, many years later.

Liz remained busy making mountains of bread that, as she said, "I wrapped in some sort of waxed paper and sold in town. I also sold my bread to the army during the war. They came in a wagon and got it. I made bread for 'my family' too, the Indians in Robin's Nest." She also made a good steady income from sewing, and Little Eagle gave her money whenever he was able.

Because of her deep abiding love for Little Eagle, Liz kept pretty much to herself and had little company except Mary, her good friend and neighbor who knew everything, and later John and his family. She expressed her dislike of the town festivities and dances so she would not be expected to attend. To take part in the dancing and parties would have been tantamount to presenting herself as a single, available widow, and she had no desire to be placed in the position of having to fend off unwelcome suitors.

One night, during the war, as Little Eagle threaded his way down the path that led from Robin's Nest to Liz's back door, he encountered a Confederate sentry. Before Little Eagle could make himself known the trigger-happy soldier shot him, wounding his left eye. The injured Indian made his way to Mary's house (the path he used winds right behind Mary's house), and Mary excised the bullet and bandaged his eye. He remained with Mary for several days while she nursed him back to health, and they did not upset Liz by telling her of this incident until it was well over.

In his early youth, John remained unaware of who his real father was. Liz did not tell him that his father was Indian. She said: "Little Eagle told John the truth when he was about eight years old. Little Eagle came, took John into the woods, and taught him what the Wise One had taught Little Eagle. They spent a lot of time together after that." John grew to love and respect his father very deeply.

## MARY

One of the first friends Liz made when she moved into Millboro was Mary. Mary's house was located across the road from the house that Little Eagle had bought for Liz.

Linda Roberts Ross is the daughter of Barbara Roberts, and she lives about an hour's drive from Lake Elsinore. When she was first regressed back to the time of the American Civil War, she gave her

**"MARY"**

*Linda Roberts Ross, born in Torrance, CA, 1956,*
*oldest daughter of Barbara Roberts. Married since 1974 to*
*Michael Ross; mother of four children.*
*Currently part-owner/manager of business*
*in Norwalk, CA.*

name as Mary and said: "I'm by myself walking down a road, going into town, to the market. I need sugar and flour to make some bread and cakes. I am in my mid twenties and have not been married long. My husband's name is Steven. He is very funny, silly all the time, and I'm crazy about him. We live on about thirty-five acres of land that I inherited from my father. I was my father's oldest daughter, but they didn't like women to inherit property then. The property and ranch is just outside of Millboro so I could walk to town. There are lots of pine trees and rolling hills. The house is nice and has a big porch. It's a horse ranch. The war is not close by; it bothers me but hasn't personally affected me yet."

When asked about "Marlboro" she started to laugh: "Oh, did they change the name?" Mary was one of the few that called it Millboro. She claimed: "It's a pretty town; it feels real peaceful and there's big trees all along the road. The town is a mix of people, lots of nationalities." Prior to the start of the war, Millboro had been peopled almost exclusively with those of English descent, but that was all rapidly changing.

Going ahead in time she said: "Things are bad—the war is still going on and things are hard. I am living alone; Steven went away to fight and I couldn't keep the farm. They kept taking my horses!! Because they were fine horses, the soldiers would notice them as they came into town and they would requisition them. I had a small buggy which I kept hidden in the barn. The soldiers' horses would be worn out, tired and not shod, so they would take mine. I had the best horses in town."

Mary made a little money selling her eggs to the man who owned the mercantile. She said: "He was a big, white-haired man. He wants the North to win. I want to say his name is Walsh." I told her to look at the sign on the store and she said: "Yes, it says C.W. Walsh Mercantile." Actually it was W.C. Warren. Mr. Warren talked politics all the time and was openly in favor of the North. Mary guessed nothing happened to him because they all needed the store so badly, but his views were unpopular with almost everyone.

She said with pain in her voice: "There were a lot of people traveling through the town during the war. I had so much trouble by myself, keeping people off my land. They just wouldn't stay off. It got dangerous. They found out I was by myself so I had to leave. Steven was gone and I couldn't keep the farm. They took my dad's land!!" This last was said in an anguished tone.

After losing her property, Mary headed northeast to a big town. She said: "It was not safe for me to stay. I went up north to Baltimore and was there a couple of years. I was very good with numbers and worked in a store doing the accounts. The job paid well for a woman. I was trying to earn enough money to go home and get my land back." Tenaciously she clung to her goal of saving enough money to go back to Millboro and reclaim her land. This was her driving force and the motivation that kept her going through those grim, unhappy years.

## BECKY

Becky was the kind of person often described as "a cute kid." There was always something charmingly childish about her even though she had borne eight of her own children by the time she died. She had a trim figure and long brownish hair with highlights that gleamed golden in the sunlight. Becky was proud of her beautiful hair; she loved to wear it long and flowing down past her shoulders. At the time when she lived, however, it was considered a little wanton for a woman to wear her hair loose and free. Women, especially married women, were expected to wear their hair up and pinned to their heads.

Maureen, according to others in my study, bears quite a physical resemblance to Becky. Maureen has naturally brown hair that she highlights to a shiny blonde. Both have large round eyes and their figures are similar.

Becky was born somewhere around 1835, in Herndon, Virginia. She was the middle of three sisters; Christine was the oldest, then Rebeccah or Becky, as she was usually called, and Allison the youngest. Unfortunately, the woman who regressed into the life of Christine found her life at that time too emotionally upsetting to continue participating in the research. Although she still finds it fascinating, after several interesting sessions she decided not to continue to be involved and requested anonymity. It is understandable that some people would find emotions back in Millboro

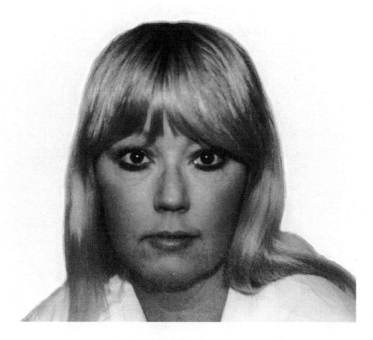

## "BECKY"

*Maureen Williamson, formerly Gremling,*
*born in Boston, MA, 1950.*
*Moved to Long Beach, CA, at the age of four.*
*Has lived in Lake Elsinore since 1970.*
*Had never been to Virginia when this study began.*

that they would prefer not to re-experience. Everyone involved in the study on a long-term basis experienced a wide range of demanding emotions. The 1860s were not a tranquil time for the people of Millboro, as the Civil War raged around them and their lives intertwined in an increasingly complex way.

When Christine described her sister Becky, she said: "She's fun loving, warm, and friendly. She has long brown hair, blue eyes, and freckles." Their father ran the blacksmith shop in Herndon, and the girls spent a lot of time there. Christine recalled: "We have fun in the shop. It's warm there and it's good company. Lots of people in and out, lots of laughs." Smiling, Christine said of Becky: "She jumps around a lot, talks a lot, and gets in the way. She's a pest!" Christine's love for her little sister was obvious, and it was partly this love that made the regression so painful later on. Christine described herself: "I have brown hair and green eyes. I am taller than Becky and much more of a lady! Becky is like a tomboy." Allison, the youngest sister, was rarely found in their father's shop with the other two girls; she had more serious interests. Becky said: "She likes to look at butterflies; she sticks them on a board. I can see her running through the fields with a net. She loved to catch butterflies and moths as well. She would sit with a glass jar and put it right over the bugs to catch them."

Becky was a blithe, unfettered spirit. Her biggest problem as a young girl seemed to be the hated long skirts. Christine said: "They wind up on her." Becky's dress would inevitably twist it's way up to her knees before her father would notice and call out to her to pull it down. Becky complained: "It's way too big! It's worse when I have to wear underskirts beneath it!"

One day a young man came into the blacksmith's shop. Becky said: "I was with my father at the shop, just sitting there. I was thirteen. The man brought his horse in; he lived in Millboro. I thought he was cute. He took me fishing and I showed him where I got the trout and bigmouth." He noticed her also, and a powerful attraction began to grow between them. His name was John Daniel Aushlick, which sounds like Ashford.

John had grown up to be a healthy, handsome man and became some sort of lawman (the accounts differ slightly). When asked what John did for a living, Becky replied proudly: "He's the sheriff." Others in the study had referred to him as "constable" and "under sheriff." In any case, he was a lawman of some sort and apparently well liked in town. When he and Becky met that day at her father's blacksmith shop, the attraction was immediate. Their affections grew as they shared more and more time together, fishing and taking long walks in the countryside. A couple of years after they met, Becky recalled: "John asked my father if he could marry me. Father didn't want to lose me, but he loved John and thought marriage was a great idea."

So Becky and John were married. When I regressed them together, Becky and her sister Christine described the wedding. Becky said: "It was in a church. Christine is crying." Christine said: "It's sad. It's not jealousy; weddings are beautiful." Becky added: "She cries all the time. My sisters were the bridesmaids. Jeff, John's cousin, was John's best man. John lived in Millboro, and none of us girls had ever been to Millboro. I will like Millboro because John will be with me." Asked if she was looking forward to the honeymoon, Becky answered: "Oh, yes. I'm definitely looking forward to the honeymoon." She added coyly that she and John had done a little fooling around before they were married. We agreed that it's hard to stay apart when they knew that they would soon be married.

Laughingly Becky confided: "When it was time for me to be a woman, my mother told me I would have to bleed because of Eve. For a long time I hated Eve! Then my mother said that there are things you have to do when you are married. She said, 'Just pretend, just lay there and let him do it and then just go and wash!'" Giggling and shaking her head, Becky continued: "I never told her we had so much fun! I wasn't supposed to like it, but I just did. We used to go by the river and back into the woods. It was always fun!" Then with Becky's own type of reasoning she concluded: "That's why it didn't hurt so much when the babies were born."

This bit of information came out of the second hypnosis session I had with Maureen and proved central to understanding Becky's character. She was a happy-go-lucky, fun loving girl, and to her, making love was the best fun there was. Fun that was eventually to prove her undoing in a terrible way.

In Millboro, according to Becky, she and John had "a little sort of ranch." It was located on the outskirts of the town, off the main road and in the direction of the town of Warm Springs. Their house was surrounded on three sides by beautiful woods with a bubbling creek running through it. In the front of the house was a large clearing that ran from the house up to the main road. They had a barn behind the house with chickens, cows, and various other domestic animals, and they raised a great deal of their own food. The water in the creek out back was clear and sweet, Becky said: "I kept a graniteware cup tied over by the spring so that the kids wouldn't have to come in the house for a drink."

Becky learned to cook with great skill, and one of her specialties was carrot cake, John's favorite treat. "When I made the cake I would use carrots, grating them (making a grating motion with her left hand), but sometimes when I'm in a hurry I'd just chew them, then spit them out and wash them. You have to wash them off real good if you chew them." Becky explained this all so matter-of-factly: "Then I mix them together with the flour and spice. It's what John likes so much!" One has to bear in mind that we are listening to a highly unsophisticated, sparingly educated, young teenage bride who lived in the back hills of Virginia in the 1850s. However, so strongly did Becky associate the spicy taste of carrot cake with John, that 130 years later, eating a piece of it would bring his name, or a name very similar, into the mind of Maureen.

Becky and John had a great deal of fun together, and babies started coming almost immediately. In all, they had eight children, five of which survived, a not uncommon statistic for the time. When Becky told me about the babies that had died, her voice grew shaky and her eyes filled with tears: "We tried to keep them warm, but they got stiff; they got stiff and were shaking." She and John would put the sick babies between them in bed in an attempt to keep them warm, but all efforts to save them failed, and the three that were taken sick succumbed, one at a time. There were three tiny, white wooden crosses in the yard between the house and the barn. The five surviving children were Phoebe, the oldest, then Robert, Rachael, Elizabeth, and later baby Peter. Becky had said that her oldest child's name was Phoebe, but later others disclaimed this, insisting that the child's name was Priscilla.

The older children helped a lot, Priscilla with the cooking and Robert with the milking. Robert was mentioned frequently during the telling of this story by all participants. He was reputed to be an unusually gifted artist and drew many sketches, focusing on the Civil War when he was very young. All the children were very hale and hearty except Robert. His bones were small and he was weaker, suffering a lot from the croup.

The sewing machine had just barely been invented by this time, but no one in Millboro had ever heard of it, much less deigned to own one. Becky proudly described making clothing for herself and her family: "I get broadcloth from the general store and tracings, markings, then make a pattern. We have to make the pattern out of the paper they wrap the fabric in. I cut them, pin them, then sew them by hand—very little stitches." She used something like a rug beater to wash clothes. When encouraged to draw a picture of it, it appeared to be a large metal loop that was secured to a wooden handle. She used this tool to push the clothing through the water and to pull the wet clothes out of the water. The washing was done in a big metal tub out in the yard near the area where she made her own soap. The soap was made at the edge of the woods because, she explained: "It stinks!" She also made cheese that she hung in the basement to age.

The family meals consisted of oatmeal and bacon for breakfast, and on Sunday they had eggs. There was no juice to drink, because they had no fruit trees, but for special treats they had pancakes. For lunch they ate a lot of chicken, grouse, and biscuits. Stew was a frequent mainstay for dinner and, of course, the beloved carrot cake.

In one session Becky was asked if there were hot springs near Millboro and replied: "There's sulphur springs, a lot of them. There's small ones and there's big ones. There are no buildings around; the springs are just out in the woods." I asked if she and John play around in the sulphur water. She laughed: "We got the first baby on the river, on the shore. We were fishing and one thing led to another . . . it always does. We fooled around in the hot springs as long as no one was there. There's trees around the springs and sometimes we wear nothing, because it's hot and it feels good. You can't go in winter—it's too cold."

On a recent trip to Millboro, Maureen, Smokey (another character in the study), and I set out to locate the spa area containing the sulphur pools. Driving to what is now Millboro Springs (in the 1800s it was called Old Millboro, because it was near the mill), Becky was tranced and led us to the general area of the pools. We searched to no avail, then we learned, to our dismay and disgust, that some years back the highway department filled in all three of the sulphur artesian pools and built a highway over them!

Going on, Becky said: "In the summer we all bathed in the river, and in the winter we have a tub that hangs outside. We bring the tub inside and heat the water outside. I bathe a lot. They said at church that we have to bathe once a week, but that's just not enough!"

Although Becky seemed familiar with scripture—possibly because biblical text was often used for reading lessons in school—she was not particularly fond of church. As a squirmy, active youngster she found having to sit still for the length of a church service was torture, and it bored her senseless. When older she had definite views on Christianity and orthodox religion. She vehemently disapproved of communion, stating: "It's like savages! If someone died for you, you don't eat them!" They held communion at her church, but she adamantly avoided it.

Becky was asked to describe the holidays. She replied: "At Thanksgiving we get together with a lot of our neighbors. Sometimes it's at the church. There's a great long table. We all cook something; it's a community affair. Christmas is at home. We decorate the tree with berries and popcorn. We use candles all the time, but you can't put them near the tree. One year John made me a beautiful cradle out of wood; it was so pretty. I sewed two slips of leather together to make him a sort of pouch to hold his badge when he was not wearing it. Sometimes we celebrate in the barn. On Guy Fawkes Day, it's in the barn." It soon became clear that the festive highlight of the whole year was Guy Fawkes Day.

It was really pretty funny—Maureen in trance as Becky had been going on and on about Guy Fawkes Day. She just loved Guy Fawkes Day, being the outgoing girl that she was. She described how everyone cooked for days and days—pies, turkeys, ham, grouse, potatoes, and all kinds of foods—and the games, the dancing, everything. But the first thing she said to me when she came out of trance was: "Who the heck was Guy Fawkes?" It reminded me of another session when she was describing with gusto the foods that they liked to eat then. When she came out of the trance she said: "What the heck are grouse?" This Guy Fawkes Day seemed really strange, because that was an English celebration, and why would a little town in Virginia be celebrating that holiday? It wasn't all that far from revolutionary times, and one would think they wouldn't have wanted anything to do with an English holiday.

Upon checking it was discovered that, sure enough, Guy Fawkes was a British revolutionary who plotted to blow up the King and both Houses of Parliament in 1605. He was discovered and hanged, and ever since then the British have celebrated his execution by hanging him, in effigy, every November 5th. Becky described the festivities as starting outside but ending up in the barn, because as evening approached, she said: "It got too cold to stay outdoors. It was right after harvest." Nearly everyone in my study mentioned this celebration; it was obviously a very important part of Millboro life, at least before the war. Barbara Roberts as Liz provided the answers.

She said: "The Guy Fawkes Day celebration in Millboro was not endemic to the South then; it was an isolated instance. A small group of the British-descended 'elite' in town decided to have their own exclusive holiday. Because of the large bonfire, it had to be held outdoors, and it was not long before, uninvited, the entire town joined in. It was held right after the harvest when everyone was in the mood for a good party. Halloween was not celebrated then as it is today. People shied away from it because Halloween had evolved from the early days of witchcraft, and there was mystery and superstition associated with it."

According to Becky, the festivities started late in the afternoon: "There's a bonfire when it's dark and we dance around it. There's lots of music, fiddles and harmonica. We have dinner; there is lots of food. Everybody bakes food for days, pies, ham, turkey, and cakes. There was liquor way in the back, but just the men go out there." Women were not supposed to drink the corn liquor, but adventuresome Becky had tasted it at some time because, she said, making a face: "It's pretty fiery!"

There were games for the kids, Becky recalled: "They roll potatoes with a stick and they win a pie. The girls have a game with clothespins. They drop them into a jar and the one that gets the most in wins. There is also a sack race." But the highlight of the day was the hanging of a large straw effigy—Guy Fawkes—immediately followed by a huge bonfire. Liz would have been happy to cancel the entire event, she explained: "The older boys would get too out of hand and make fools of themselves. They ran wild and nobody makes them mind. They played in the fire and would use the burning sticks like they were swords. It was dangerous, especially with the little ones around." Liz herself never attended. This was partly because as a single or widowed woman, her presence at the party would have made her seem available, and she remained steadfastly true to Little Eagle in every way. When John was young, she also tried everything in her power to keep him away from it, but with little success.

Except for the tragic deaths of the three babies, John, Becky, and their family seemed to have an ideal life in Millboro prior to the outbreak of the Civil War. In ways both direct and indirect, the war signalled the advent of personal disasters from which none of them ever really recovered. While John and Becky both loved each other very much, they each became entwined in romantic affairs outside their marriage that had devastating consequences.

While attending a party at a social club in Lake Elsinore several months ago, a man got up to leave the room and walked right past me. The feeling that went through me defies description—it was like a jolt of electricity, the hair rising on the back of my neck. Starting out of my chair, the thought roared through my mind: "That's John!" There had never even been a picture in my mind of what John looked like—I just knew this was him! Seeking out Barbara Roberts, who was there with me, I ordered: "Take a look at that man over there." Barbara reacted as though she was going to faint. Turning white as a sheet she said: "That's John!" She'd never met the man, never even laid eyes on him until that moment.

Barbara, who regressed back to Liz, was John's mother in Millboro, so it was quite an emotional moment for her. We both just sat there with our mouths open.

Everyone in this work seems to agree that this man in Lake Elsinore, who we identified as John, looks more like his counterpart than anyone else in the group.

## CONSTANCE & AVA

Constance came to the study in the person of Nancy (not her real name), who lives in a town near Lake Elsinore and knows Maureen. When Maureen first began experiencing the life of Becky, one of the first people she saw there was Constance. As soon as Becky came out the trance she said: "That's Nancy!"

Alice (not her real name) came to my study through Maureen and Nancy; she is a friend of both women. Alice regressed back to Ava, Constance's mother. Alice was present at the first session held with Constance and Becky when they were regressed together. Later, when Alice was regressed to the lifetime of Ava, it became obvious that something was not right. Her replies were disjointed; she kept her hand over her mouth most of the time, and her answers were vague and obtuse. She made it clear that she did not like that lifetime, was unhappy throughout most of it, and did not want to be there. She hated and feared her husband, Constance's father, but obviously adored Constance and Becky. She said: "I just have my own life inside that nobody knows about." When I asked her if she was lonely, she answered: "Yes, except for Constance."

Shortly after Becky moved to Millboro, she met Constance Waverly. The two girls were close in age and soon became fast friends. Constance was rich, spoiled, and could often be a venomous little snip, but Becky was blissfully unaware of it and went out of her way to impress and entertain Constance and Ava. In terms of wealth and position, Constance's family far outranked that of Becky's, but Becky's home life had been much more happy and stable. Where Becky's father had been a blacksmith, whose shop was a hub of congenial activity, Constance's father was a powerful and controlling influence in town, very conscious of his own importance, authoritarian and cold toward his family. Where Becky had grown up as a giggling tomboy, with sisters to play with and much activity to be part of, Constance was to all intent and purpose an only child, isolated in a large lonely house with servants, a father she rarely saw, and a mother everyone considered unbalanced. (There was one vague mention of some "other girl in the house" who passed through—this became clear later—and a brief reference to a dead brother, who was apparently long gone by the time Becky moved to Millboro.) Becky was a breath of fresh, sweet air to Constance and Ava, and what she lacked in class she more than made up for in her high-spirited enjoyment of life.

Nancy turned out to be excellent under hypnosis, and a lot of information and insight were obtained from her. When Becky and Constance were regressed together, they just turned into giggling schoolgirls. They were hilarious! Becky loved to be outrageous for Constance and Ava, and she'd play the clown for them. In the presence of Constance, Becky's personality became much more brash; you could tell she took great delight in shocking her and Ava, and they both just loved it! They were so bored in that little town with their big house and servants, and Becky was such a ham. The bigger the audience she got, the more she acted up, not unlike Maureen today.

Constance immediately changed demeanor when she was with Becky. Her voice became high pitched, and she laughed and giggled incessantly. The least thing said, no matter how inconsequential, would throw both girls into peals of uncontrollable laughter.

Mr. Waverly, Constance's father, was a town leader: "In politics, father once held an office in town. They didn't have a mayor. There's a general committee; he headed the committee once." Becky added: "He buys the politicians. He has money."

At fifteen, Constance remembered: "My father made me marry Garrett. He was my father's friend; they are both in politics. Garrett's a lot older than me and he's terrible. My husband and my father make a good pair—they should marry each other." Becky's observation about Garrett was more succinct: "He's stuffed!" Constance said: "Father hates Becky. Garrett really hates her! They think Becky is a bad influence on me." But since neither Constance's father nor her husband were home much, and since there was absolutely no one else in Millboro who wanted to spend time with Constance, the two men soon abandoned their attempts to keep the two girls apart. Most of the time Becky met Constance at her house while Garrett was at work.

The house that Mr. Waverly had built for Constance and Garrett stood right in the middle of Millboro, up the hill a short distance from a railroad tunnel known as Katy's Tunnel. Becky's house was further out, on the edge of town. The girls soon found a shortcut through the woods, so that they could visit each other easily.

Becky recalled that she had both a dog and a cat. She did not think the cat had a name, but the dog was named Bruno. Constance had a dog too, and Becky interrupted to state disparagingly: "He's a fancy dog." Constance's dog was named Duncan, and he was a big, white, long-haired, sissy-looking dog.

Constance had flaming red hair (as does Nancy today) and according to Becky, "has to have rags in her hair all the time to make it curly. I only put rags in my hair sometimes, for very special occasions." When Constance was asked whether she wore her hair up or down, she replied indignantly: "I am supposed to wear it up. Oh, that's the way they like it, more ladylike, older. I like to wear it down. Garrett likes it up. He says you shouldn't flaunt your beauty, that men shouldn't look at you when you are married."

Constance described her clothes: "I wear long dresses and sometimes hats. I don't really like hats because they are hot in the summer." Constance's mother, Ava, was known not only for her erratic behavior, but also for a hat she wore that was the talk of the town. It was mentioned several times. When Ava was asked to describe her hat, she replied: "It was some of the smoothest grey stuff. It was smoother than felt and there was ribbon on it." Becky chimed in: "It came from Philadelphia, from the book." Ava said she had a special outfit that went with her grey hat: "Oh, the dress was beautiful; the color was grey. It was a winter dress. I did not

*Ava's hat.*
*Sketched by Joe while entranced as Charley*

get the dress through the catalog. I have a dressmaker in town, Mrs. Tuttle, who made it for me." Ava's grey outfit was talked about for weeks. In addition to being well dressed, she was a stunningly beautiful woman, although terribly unhappy. When we were searching for Ava's name, Constance suggested facetiously: "Mrs. Waverly." That was the only name her father ever used with his wife, even when they were alone. Constance continued with: "Mrs. Waverly was his favorite possession!" Asked what Ava's grandchildren called her, Constance quickly answered: "Mrs. Waverly" amid hoots of laughter from the Becky and Ava. Then Constance declared as an afterthought: "My mother has no name."

Constance too was unhappy much of the time, trapped in a marriage with a much older man. She said that Garrett was condescending toward her: "He looks at me and calls me 'little girl.'" Becky added: "She is scared of Garrett. She would never stand up to him on anything. He gets belligerent and nasty and he hits her sometimes. He is very sanctimonious and she is unhappy with him." Constance said: "Becky is my salvation. She makes me laugh at Garrett."

Shortly after the war started, Millboro was overrun with Confederate soldiers, sent there to guard the two railroad tunnels and the huge piles of supplies that were rapidly growing all over the town. Constance and Becky said they were told it was an honor and privilege to have the soldiers among them and that they should treat the soldiers well. It appears that Becky stayed away from the men in uniform, but with Constance it was a different story. Constance became involved with a Lieutenant Orr, who was in charge of ordinance in Millboro at the time. Constance was known at times for her sadistic sense of humor. Once she set Becky up so that Becky would walk in and catch herself and Lt. Orr "en flagrante delicto," an occasion that upset and offended Becky terribly. Rationalizing their behavior, one could observe that there was very little in the line of entertainment in Millboro in the mid 1800s, and obviously the girls found their own way of alleviating their everyday boredom.

One never ending source of hilarity to them both was Becky's affair with Charley, a man in town who trained horses. Constance giggled: "Charley is always falling down. He might have a bad leg, but he drinks a lot." Becky agreed and admitted: "I like it when he falls down." Constance laughing: "You would!" Constance suggested that made it easier to jump on Charley, and Becky replied dryly: "It's not hard anyway." Constance continued: "There is a bar in Millboro. I never go in, but Becky goes in sometimes. Becky just likes to have fun. She says she doesn't go there, but I know she does. They wouldn't serve her, not in front of everybody. John doesn't go in there, but Charley does. Everybody knows about them." Finally Becky, needing to retaliate, announced: "Constance smokes a little ivory pipe!" "Becky you promised!!!" Constance exclaimed with utter contempt.

Another great source of mirth was an underwear salesman named Derrick. Constance said: "All men are part of Becky's problem, because Charley's not the only one in her life." Both girls giggled uncontrollably. Constance continued: "There's a man named Derrick. He comes into the store every three or four months. Becky likes him; he's very handsome. He sells underwear." Derrick definitely had something going with one of the girls. At first the insinuation was that Becky was attracted to him, but later it came out that it was really Constance. Apparently when Constance became involved with Derrick, she very cleverly told him that her name was Becky and that her husband was the lawman in town. This prank would have been harmless except Derrick liked to talk too much, and he bragged to the porter on the train, who in turn soon spread the gossip all over the saloon in Millboro. This was just one more bit of tarnish on Becky's already blemished reputation.

Derrick gave Constance several items of the latest styles in women's undergarments, which she dared not keep so she promptly turned them over to Becky. One was a white lace corselette that fit up under the bust and laced up the back. It was really more of a waist cincher. Since it was too large, even when tightly laced, it was of no use to Becky. The second item was a white, knit union suit that buttoned down the front and in the crotch. It was sleeveless and stopped just above her knees, but it was nice and warm, and Becky loved it in the cold weather. The highlight of Becky's underwear windfall was a pair of pantaloons, which she persisted in calling "bloomers." They were long, white cotton pants with rows of ruffles from the knees down to the ankles. Pretty and feminine, she felt very dressed up when wearing them. Becky did not own a hoop skirt, but all her dresses were long, and when wearing the bloomers, she would flip up her skirt at the slightest provocation, revealing rows of white ruffles.

Becky was clearly the more domestic of the two, sewing all the clothes for herself and her family, while Constance had most of her clothes made for her. Becky was a good cook and enjoyed it;

Constance had servants to cook for her. Becky also spent a great deal of time canning and putting up preserves, with Constance watching in fascinated interest. They both described in some detail the white cheese that Becky made. They were careful to state it was not cottage cheese, which they both hated then and still do today. Becky started: "You put the milk in a big jar." Constance added: "You put that screen on it." Becky continued: "That's when I have to pour it in and then all of the whey comes out. Then, when it gets in a lump in there, I have to thump it out. After I get it strained, I run it through the screen, then I put it in the cloth and hang it underneath." Constance interrupted: "You have to tie that cloth. You tie it up and it has to go underneath the house where it's dark, in the basement. You leave it there a month or so." Becky said: "It's made from both cow's milk and goat's milk. I like goat's milk cheese better; it's sweeter."

Sometimes Becky would pack a lunch and she and Constance would walk out into the woods, collecting wildflowers. Occasionally they took all their kids with them, but usually they went alone. On rare occasions they would ride horses, but Becky said with disgust: "Constance is not allowed to get dirty. Her husband does not like her to do anything!" This put a crimp in a lot of activities for Constance, perhaps including attending Guy Fawkes Day. Constance was one of the few subjects in my study that had no recollections of the Guy Fawkes celebrations, and considering their rowdy nature and Garrett's iron hand, she most likely was not allowed to attend.

On these outings there was a lot of daydreaming about new, different, and exciting lives. They both recalled: "Once we made plans to run away. We didn't do it, oh no, but someday maybe we would have, way over the hills to California. We would even walk. We weren't planning to take our kids. We can get more kids—we do a good job with that. We were going to watch the sun in California and dig for gold. We wouldn't have to work; we'd just let the boys out West entertain us. We would love that!!"

Sometimes on their sojourns they would encounter one of the many stills that were hidden in those hills. They were never frightened and claimed that the still operators were friendly to them. Becky said: "They would offer us a drink." This is apparently how Becky had gotten her taste of the well-talked-about corn liquor.

When Becky, Constance, and Ava were hypnotized together, the conversation was directed toward Constance's housekeeper, whom they all despised and made fun of at every opportunity. Constance stated adamantly: "She's terrible! She's mean to everybody!" Garrett hired her, and he liked her because she exercised strong discipline in the household, and it was his attitude that they all needed control. Constance was scared of her, Becky loathed her and considered the entire situation ridiculous, and Ava just thought it was funny. They all had their pet names for her, but the favorite was "Beulah Blackbottom." Whenever this name was mentioned, they would all three roar with laughter. Beulah Blackbottom was a name the kids made up for the housekeeper, whose real name was Lydia. Behind her back they drew ugly, unflattering pictures of her, made up names to call her, and executed a derogatory gesture by placing a hand over their nose and making a downward motion with it. Then Ava volunteered: "I call her Mrs. Toad" and all three again shook with laughter. "Robert touched her once and he got a wart," piped up Becky.

Ava was described by Becky and Constance as petite, with very thick, dark, wavy hair, a small face, and dark eyes—not unlike the way Alice looks today. Ava's husband was very proud of the fact that she was so good-looking. "She is one of his possessions," Constance snorted derisively, "like a prize cow." A lot of the women in town were jealous of Ava, despite her obvious dementia, because of her youthful beauty and her role as the town fashion plate, as evidenced by the famous grey outfit.

Late one night, Ava's house burned down. This happened shortly after her husband had died. It was widely believed that Ava had set it on fire herself, and when asked if she had really done this, she smiled enigmatically and stated: "It would not have been too difficult." When asked if Ava was capable of doing this, Becky replied: "Maybe." Why would she do such a thing, I wondered, and

Becky said: "She hated the house, because she hated her husband so much." The townspeople joined together in an attempt to try to control the fire, but their efforts were useless. Their only means of fire fighting was a bucket brigade, desperately hauling pails of water from the creek behind the house. Not only did Ava's house burn to the ground, but many of the trees surrounding the house burned also.

It seems that Constance's father had been involved in some sort of black magic or devil worship cult that met in an area referred to as "Top Woods" in nice weather and in Mr. Waverly's basement when the weather was inclement. According to the three, there was an altar in the basement used for sacrificing small animals and a large meeting room where the rituals were conducted. Ava said: "Sometimes there was evil in that house," and Constance added: "She wanted to get rid of the evil." Becky said, "She had to make sure that no one ever lived there again, because of things that happened there. They were very bad, and she knew what she had to do. She had to do it."

Becky later stated separately that she thought it was possible that Mr. Waverly secretly doped Ava up from time to time in order to deliberately cause her erratic behavior. That way if she ever had made any statements about his clandestine activities, she would never have been believed.

Constance and Becky once sneaked up the hillside after dark to the Top Woods area to watch one of the cult meetings. Lying on their stomachs in the tall grass, hidden among rocks and trees, they watched, frozen through an entire ritual. They said: "We saw a group of people chanting, their hands joined. Some of them were from Millboro. It's a brotherhood. Constance's father was there." Constance was not upset at seeing her father, as she knew about his activities. They watched as the group stabbed a rabbit to death and took turns drinking the blood. The girls were very nearly sick to their stomachs, but they remained still as death, flattened in the weeds, because as Becky said: "We can't go up there 'cause they'll eat us!"

The girls agreed that Ava was very artistic and drew beautiful pictures with pen and ink. They thought her drawings were possibly on display in a museum somewhere in the South.

Discussing Millboro, both girls claimed that on occasion the whole area smelled like rotten eggs due to the sulphur springs nearby. There was a barber shop in the middle of town, but they had no reason to go in there. In fact they gave it a wide berth because, as Becky said: "They did other things in there, like pull out your teeth." In those days, the barber sometimes served also as dentist and doctor. They both shuddered at the thought.

Because this life was so unpleasant to Ava, she really did not want to return to it, and Alice was unable to continue past the first several sessions.

It was with Becky and Constance that the psychic ramifications of this type of hypnosis were revealed. Together they stated that Elizabeth, one of Becky's daughters, had lived in Becky and John's house after they were gone. When she left, the house stood empty for a long time and eventually burned down. They continued saying that now a tall white church stands where Becky's house had been. The church has steep steps in front, a tall tower with a blue window, and large grey bricks on the bottom.

Constance's house was still standing, they concurred, but it had been painted a different color. It had been brown with grey trim; now it was yellow with green trim. It was in very good shape and looked as though more than one family lived there. They stated that the clearing was all that was left of Ava's house; nothing had been built there since the fire. When we went to Millboro, a few months later, we discovered that these observations were startlingly true.


## CHARLEY

It was clear from the earliest regressions with Maureen going back to the life of Becky, that the story didn't stop with her. During the very first session, after coming up out of the trance, Maureen said: "I saw a whole bunch of people there. Joe's back there . . . I

*"CHARLEY"*

*Joe Nazarowski, born in Chicago, IL, 1947.*
*Attended high school in Anaheim, CA. Served in U.S. Army*
*1964–67 in Viet Nam, 1970–72 in Marine Corps,*
*stationed in U.S. Extensive background in law enforcement.*
*Prior to Millboro study, had never been to Virginia.*
*Also known as "Peter."*

could see Joe very clearly." Not knowing who she was talking about, I asked: "Joe who?" and she said: "Joe Nazarowski," a man she knew in Lake Elsinore. Being absolutely intrigued, I was delighted when she brought him over with her the next time. At first Joe was individually regressed, then later the two of them were hypnotized together, and when that was done, the story that emerged was much clearer.

A year or two into the war, Charley Morgan came to the town of Millboro. Most of the people in the study refer to him as Charley, but Becky said: "I called him Peter because the minister told us about Saint Peter, how his church was built upon a rock, because he was so strong. Charley was strong like a rock too."

Charley described himself as a cavalry officer who was wounded at the battle of Shiloh and, after a medical discharge from the Confederate Army, came to Millboro to train horses for the Confederacy. He had been regular army and had graduated from West Point at just about the time that the Civil War broke out. He chose Millboro, he said, "because it was directly on the railroad line and would be easy to ship trained horses to the front lines."

Millboro in fact was the turnaround point for the Central Virginia Railroad. There was a tunnel through which the trains would pass, in order to turn around, that was referred to by nearly everyone in the story as "Katy's Tunnel." It should be explained that Katy's Tunnel was the first of two railroad tunnels that penetrated the mountains right outside of Millboro. According to my people and some of the local people in Millboro today, the tunnel was named for a "working girl" who set up shop deep in the tunnel to entertain the railroad workers while the railroad and tunnels were being built. There was a second tunnel behind Katy's, and beyond that was the turnaround where they manually turned the engine about. It was like a big carousel with no horses. This description came from Linda Ross, who regressed into the life of Mary. When I regressed Liz and Mary together, they roared with laughter. When asked how Katy's Tunnel got it's name, Mary said: "Oh God, little Katy! Everybody knew Katy or knew of her, at least all the men knew her." In order to get them talking about her, I asked what Katy did for a living—did she wait on tables? Mary replied laughing: "She waited on men! Everybody's got to make a living; what can I say? She was blonde, but I don't think the men were all that interested in her looks. She wasn't out much during the day; she slept. I'll bet the engineers had a show in that tunnel. She was crazy. If she was going to set up her little business, at least you shouldn't have had to worry about getting killed in the act! She wasn't really a bad person. People who took time to talk to her didn't think all that badly of her. She came from a bad family. She really had it hard. I think her father was just awful." Mary went on to explain that one of the men had given Katy a railroad lantern, and when she was open for business, she hung the lantern outside the tunnel. "I think it was after I left that the townspeople ran her out, Katy and her lantern. I felt sorry for her. A woman doesn't do that without being absolutely desperate." At the time this story took place, Katy was no longer in the tunnel, but her memory lingered on. The tunnel was to have great significance in Charley's life as we were to learn much later.

Under hypnosis Charley described his early life as a youth in either Ohio or Indiana. His mother had been a Southerner, and when she was widowed, she and her young son moved back to her home in Kentucky. As a young man Charley applied to West Point and lived in a torment of anxious waiting until the appointment arrived in the mail. He said: "I went to West Point almost five years. I was commissioned into the Union artillery before the end of my fifth year." His was the class of 1861, and he had a number of schoolmates who would become well known—among them George Armstrong Custer, who was in the class behind Charley. According to Charley, Custer had a sadistic sense of humor: "Custer set up a gag on a bunch of us. He strung a line or a rope across the steps in the barracks—which were cement—and when the bugle called and we ran out, we tripped. We got bumps and bruises. There were about twenty of us; four or five tripped. Custer was standing there laughing, but we got him back. We poured molasses in his boots." George Custer finished West Point last in his class, and Charley said: "Scholastically he almost didn't make it, almost didn't graduate. [He said later that Custer cheated like hell to get through.] He got poor grades, but we all helped each other." Charley continued that Custer had political aspirations (this has been established) and that he was promoted to the rank of general by his friends in Congress who went over the heads of the army brass, who disliked and mistrusted Custer and would never have made him a general.

Charley spent not quite five years at West Point and was close to graduating when the war broke out. His class was graduated early because, he said: "Both sides desperately needed officers." From West Point he was commissioned a second lieutenant in the Union Army artillery and was sent to Tennessee. He said: "I was summoned before a brigadier general who was recruiting West Pointers for the Confederate Army. I resigned my commission in the Union Army and went to some place called Wallenburg to accept a commission into the Confederate Army. I had some advanced sabre training there." Describing the identification tags that they were issued: "They were made of a real hard wood and worn around the neck on a leather thong. They had your name, religion, and a serial number printed on them in India ink." He added ruefully: "They did not last long."

An interesting aspect regarding regression hypnosis sessions is that people invariably go right back to a traumatic or important time for them in that past life. For Charley it was the battle of Shiloh. It must have been terrible. Undoubtedly it was his first big battle and he was wounded twice—once in the shoulder and once in the leg. He described the battle: "There were about two hundred men involved in the battle where I was injured. The Yankees outnumbered us and they had cannons. It was an ambush. I'm back there trying to plug up the holes in the line and to hold on. The reason my leg got injured was I saw the shell coming and realized it was going to get my horse, and my horse was my only way out of there, so I put my leg up and took the shell so it wouldn't kill my horse. After about sixty yards my horse went out from under me anyway. I was dragged by four of my men; one was a Sergeant Stuart." Later he said: "I must have had some money, because I had beautiful boots." I had been asking him about his boots and what he was wearing and later had to laugh when he told me: "I was aware of the smell of gunsmoke and I was aware of the shells. All hell was breaking loose. There's shells flying all around me, my men are getting killed right and left, the terrible noise of the cannon, and here's this woman, this voice, asking me: 'What's on your feet? What are you feeling? What are you doing now?'" He said: "I'm trying to be polite, I'm trying to talk to you, and I'm thinking, why doesn't she just go away?!!" Here Charley's in one of the biggest battles of the war, fighting for his life, and there's this little voice asking him about his boots and his sword and stuff! He certainly didn't want to talk to me at a time like that. That's how deep into it he was. That was probably his most traumatic time.

After Charley was pulled off the battlefield by his men, he said: "We went a long way away; we were in the back of a plantation. A Southern belle treated my leg; she cleaned the wound and bandaged it. We finally got back to Confederate lines and I was sent to an aid station." Charley remained at the aid station or maybe a Confederate hospital for several weeks while his wounds healed. Eventually he was declared unfit for duty and mustered out. His primary souvenir of the war was a noticeable limp.

After a short period of recuperation, Charley went to Millboro to train horses for the Confederate Army. He recalled: "I went to Millboro to train horses for the military. The horses are bred around Virginia. They're not a race horse—they are stout, good military stock, very strong. They don't need a lot of food."

Charley's horse corral was right in the middle of town, near the railroad stock loading pens. Being somewhat of a loner, he had a rather abrasive personality and never did make many friends or become involved in the community. However, he did meet John immediately after his arrival in Millboro, and they became friends. Becky claimed that John was the sheriff of Millboro, but it was learned later that Millboro never had its own sheriff. The county sheriff's office is now and was then in the town of Warm Springs. We think that John was probably an under sheriff of some sort, or perhaps a constable. Whatever his title, he was badly needed in town. The Confederate Army was rapidly infiltrating Millboro, and with it the lawless element became more abundant. Consequently, John often had his hands full and Charley was more than willing to help out, working as a deputy with John whenever trouble arose. Charley was fanatical in his devotion to the South and the Confederate cause and never missed an opportunity to air his views, usually loudly. Much later in the story it became evident that John was equally devoted to the principles of the Union, but he was wise enough to be very covert in his words and actions. Charley and John were definitely an odd couple, but they did become friends, and while John and Becky were outgoing and friendly with many, they were virtually the only friends Charley had in Millboro.

Charley's friendship with John became solid after John bought some horses from him—one of them, a horse named Shadow, was for Becky—at an exceptionally good price. After the deal was struck for the horses, John invited Charley home for dinner. This was Becky's first meeting with him. When regressed together, Charley and Becky described exactly how Becky and John's house had been laid out, where the barn stood in relation to the house, and the dinner Becky prepared: "We had chicken, corn, applesauce, and pumpkin pie."

A lot of Charley's time was spent on lengthy hunting trips, and occasionally he would be gone for days on end, sometimes to Becky's extreme annoyance. Throughout my study it became obvious that Charley's "hunting trips" were for much bigger game than the deer and rabbits that abounded in the woods. According to Warm Sun, Charley paid the Indians well with food and horse tack for information about Yankee locations. Not only were the Indians out and about, hunting, fishing, and catching wild horses in the canyons, but the location of Robin's Nest was at the top of a mountain that had a view for miles over the valley below. Warm Sun volunteered that Charley was very much afraid to go off alone on the paths throughout the woods surrounding Millboro. It seemed that those woods, as Becky and Constance told us, were full of stills and moonshiners who presented a much larger threat than any stray Yankees. The friendly Indians would check out the paths for Charley and show him how to skirt the stills. According to Warm

Sun, the moonshiners had a special graveyard where they buried federal officers and any other hapless souls who inadvertently stumbled onto their source of income.

When not engaged in training horses or off in the hills hunting, Charley spent his time gambling and drinking. He had a reputation as a heavy drinker, and according to some, he was drunk a great deal of the time. Although he did not do much socializing with the town folks, he did evidently attend some functions, such as Guy Fawkes Day, probably at Becky's prodding.

When Guy Fawkes Day was mentioned to Charley in trance, he immediately stated: "Guy Fawkes had been responsible for an attempt to kill the king and blow up Parliament." He added that a similar attempt against the president and Congress would have had his wholehearted support and that Jefferson Davis probably would also have approved such a coup.

Charley and Becky went on at some length about the food that everyone brought to the Guy Fawkes Day table, and Charley commented: "The liquor is way in the back by the trees. It's good stuff, corn liquor made here in the South. One of the boys makes it and puts it in jugs. It packs quite a punch. The women don't drink it; we never take it out to the women." At this statement Becky smiled smugly and declared: "They think we don't know."

At least eighty people attended the celebration, which started late in the afternoon and continued long into the evening. Dancing to fiddles and harmonicas rounded off the event. Charley was known to drink excessively at this event, and when asked how long the party went on, he answered matter-of-factly: "Until you fall down."

Despite his leg wound, Charley liked to dance and, according to Becky, was quite good at it. Of course all the cadets at West Point were taught dancing, among other social graces. In describing the music of the time, Charley mentioned "Turkey in the Straw," "When Johnny Comes Marching Home," and another song called "Old Rocking Horse." His all-time favorite, however, was a song he referred to as "The Chicken Song," which was a fast song with words that went: "The chicken is a scratchin', the chicken is a peckin'." Charley said: "It's a jumpy, airy tune, kind of like a Scottish tune." This "Chicken Song" came up frequently in conversations with the Millboro people. (When another character, Honey, was discovered, who operated the boarding house, she came up with a tune and more of the words.) Charley played the banjo in his off time, although by his own appraisal, not very well.

Other than the annual holidays there was not much excitement in Millboro. Once, Charley said, there was a horse race in town sponsored by a local plantation owner. Six horses ran; there was a lot of money bet and a lot of money lost. The consensus in retrospect was that the race had been fixed. That seemed to put an end to the racing fever in Millboro.

Many times Charley, as well as virtually everyone else in this study, mentioned the supplies piled up all over town and the sounds of men and clattering wagons pulling in and out of town twenty-four hours a day in a desperate attempt to supply the Confederate lines to the south and east. Since Millboro was secluded and the end point of the railroad line, it was a logical place for supplies to be unloaded, where they were then to be taken presumably to Lynchburg. But getting them out of Millboro, which had to be done by wagon, was not easy. The roads were disastrous in every season of the year. In the winter it was snow, and when it rained, especially in the spring, the roads were a sea of sticky mud, and the horses and wagons would sink a foot deep in the mire. In the dry summer the roads became such a dust bowl of deep ruts that they were practically impassable. It required so many horses and mules to haul the wagons over this difficult terrain, and they required so much feed, that there was scarcely any room left for freight.

Because there were no warehouse facilities of any kind in Millboro, at some point early in the war or possibly even before the war, an enterprising young quartermaster officer began using railroad cars for storage. He simply derailed the cars and set them to one side, filled with supplies. Eventually the Central Virginia Railroad noticed that they were operating without approximately a quarter of their cars, so an edict was sent up through the army that from that point on, arriving cars were to be unloaded immediately and sent back. That's when tents, ammunition, food, and weapons began piling up in everyone's front yards. Charley said: "The supplies were stockpiled everywhere." Toward the war's end there were mountains of supplies stacked up everywhere, around houses, all along the streets. It was a mess. Some of the food had begun to rot, and the stink was discernible all over town.

It was Charley who first mentioned that he and Becky had been lovers. Becky admitted that she had been aware of it the minute they were first hypnotized together but had just decided not to mention it. It seemed as though Becky had been the instigator in their romance. The first time they came together for a session, Charley was hypnotized and Becky was conscious. They had a short discussion about Becky's horse Shadow, then at my suggestion, Becky invited Charley over for dinner the following Saturday. Charley suspiciously asked: "Is your husband going to be there?" When Becky answered that she wasn't sure, Charley finalized the discussion with: "Well, if he is going to be there, I will come."

When Charley was discharged from the army, he was left with a wounded leg—a fairly superficial wound. Later he was seriously wounded in the same leg by one of the horses he was training. Becky spent a great deal of time with Charley, nursing his wound.

Describing how their romance got started, Charley explained: "Becky used to come to my place to treat my leg. She cleaned it out with salt water and applied a flax seed poultice to it, then she would wrap it in the cloth she put around cheese. She treated it off and on for a long time, and that is when the romance got started. We also met in several places out in the woods."

In the tender and private atmosphere of Charley's room, the romance really warmed up. Charley, periodically racked with guilt said: "I stopped it [under his breath] for a while. 'Tweren't right. John was a good man." Despite his attempts to curb the romance, it went on for a long time. Becky explained: "I don't feel it's wrong. I only have one thing that is mine, and that is myself. Peter [she always called Charley by this name] didn't take anything that wasn't his to take. We didn't steal from John." Charley added: "We always had feelings for each other."

Constance maintained that Charley drank too much and that he had been talking about his affair with Becky when he was drunk. Charley and Becky both denied this strongly, and it is certainly possible that it was actually Constance who had blabbed and, in typical fashion, was trying to place the blame somewhere else. Charley was so conscience stricken over his affair with a married woman that it's doubtful he discussed it with anyone, even when drunk. On the other hand, Becky was often less than discreet. When quizzed about her affair with Charley, Becky demanded to know who had talked and was told that Honey, the proprietor of the boarding house where Charley lived, had seen Becky sneaking into Charley's room many times. Through clenched teeth Becky replied contemptuously: "She should just bake her biscuits!"

Once, before bringing them out of trance, they were asked if either one had anything more to discuss. Becky started crying profusely and stated between tears: "He's mad at me!" Then, speaking very quickly she added: "Peter got mad at me because I took my clothes off in the woods." Charley said that he remembered getting mad at her: "She didn't use good judgement [shaking his head]. Sometimes she just throws caution to the wind. She's not always discreet—that is why I won't go to her house unless her husband is there." Although Charley was smitten with her, he was anxious and he really wanted to end the affair. Both he and Becky loved John and did not want to hurt him, but only Charley seemed to realize that would be inevitable if the affair continued.


## HONEY

Everyone loved Honey, and there was never a negative word said about her—all remarked on her generous nature and big heart. Her real name, we learned later, was Marie Elizabeth, a name she hated, so when someone started calling her Honey in her youth, the name stuck. When she was first regressed, she found herself at a party in a large house, dancing; she loved to dance. She said: "There are about twenty people here. There are some men in sort of blue

*"HONEY"*

*Millie Sproule, born in Alabama, 1928.*
*Works as office manager in family business,*
*mother of two daughters. Lives in Lake Elsinore and*
*has never been to Virginia.*

uniforms." Then in a hushed tone, she added: "I was not supposed to come to this party, but I came anyway. I came to see that man. He is not a local boy, but I have known him for quite a while. Boy, is he good-looking!" Her dancing partner was a Union soldier named Philip, and she was very taken with him. She went on rhapsodically about how much she loved to dance and what songs she liked. When it was casually mentioned that one of the men in the group liked "The Chicken Song," she became very animated and exclaimed: "Oh we go 'round and 'round to that one!" At a later time she sang it:

Chicken in the bread basket
Scratchin' out the dough
Honey does your dog bite?
No, chile, no!

The dance was being held at a very large plantation-type house with pillars out in front. They had removed all the furniture from the room in order to have the dance. It was obviously just prior to the outbreak of hostilities, and secrecy was of the utmost importance because of the many Union soldiers who were attending. Devotees of the Union cause were not popular in the South even before the Civil War.

The handsome Philip went off to war while Honey stayed in Millboro and remained in an unhappy marriage with a man named Thomas Mason. Thomas was a gambler, and in a poker game he had won a large boarding house that stood then (and still does) in the middle of Millboro. Later, Thomas was killed when caught cheating in a card game. Honey recalled: "He was shot by some men he was gambling with over in Cedar Creek. He and his sidekick, Hoppy Harper, had been sent to Cedar Creek by John (Becky's husband) to get some gun powder." All that was learned about Hoppy is that he was a part-time fur trader who did odd jobs for Thomas. He was a cheerful person who persisted in wearing a large, well-worn fur coat even in the warmest weather. Hoppy bathed infrequently, if at all, and was difficult to be near for any length of time. He stayed to himself quite a bit and wore, in addition to the fur coat, a hat with a large feather in it. He was not popular in town, but Honey liked him, because he sensed her unhappiness with her marriage, and he would play the fiddle and sing to her when she was depressed.

Not exactly plunged into grief over the demise of Thomas, Honey's only comment was: "He was a sorry husband and I didn't love him. He wasn't around the kids much." She was left with the boarding house and two little girls, aged seven and two. Martha, the oldest girl, died in a drowning accident shortly after her father was shot, and the baby, Marie, died in the terrible epidemic that swept through Millboro right after the war.

Much to her shock and amazement, soon after Thomas died, Honey discovered stacks of money in his office. She said: "It was Confederate money. I found it in Thomas's desk and I changed it to gold and put it in the bank. Between the money and the boarding house I lived in relative comfort."

According to Honey's descriptions of the boarding house, the ground floor was a large restaurant with a small bar at the rear and a good-sized kitchen off to one side in the back. Upstairs she had several large rooms that she rented out. There were several smaller rooms on a third floor, some of which she rented out and some of which she provided to her help. Honey ran the house and did all the cooking for the restaurant. She had a reputation as not only a compassionate, friendly woman, but also as an excellent cook, a hard worker, and a very shrewd businesswoman.

Charley lived in Honey's boarding house during his years in Millboro. Honey liked him but said: "He drank way too much, especially toward the end. He's loud and he laughs a lot. He got a leg injury in the war; that's why he limps." She thought he was good-looking and said: "He was nice to me, always a real gentleman."

Regarding Becky: "Becky's a cute girl. She has a bunch of kids and lives out of town a little bit. I see her when she comes into town. She comes to my rooming house and sneaks in to see Charley." Asked why it was necessary for Becky to sneak around, Honey hissed: "She's married! Her husband is the under sheriff." She explained that the boarding house had stairs outside, on both sides of the building, which make it easy for anyone to enter and exit the bedrooms above unobserved—or so they thought.

When Honey was regressed with Becky and Liz, they all started talking about Katy's Tunnel. Honey said: "It's dark in there. Was she a floozy?" All three started laughing. Becky said: "Yes, she was a floozy. They named the tunnel for her because that's where she conducted business." Asked if Katy conducted her business with the railroad crew, all three answered: "With anybody!!" and laughed more. They said Katy had a bed of straw back in the tunnel and she would entertain the men back there. Liz said: "They would watch for her light." Honey added: "She was run out of town."

Then they talked about the bank in Millboro. Honey answered: "Yeah, I've got gold there. The bank is down and across the street from my boarding house." Becky announced: "I don't have any money!" She didn't have to worry about the bank. Liz added: "There's something else there too; it's the telegraph office." They said the bank had never been robbed. Liz said proudly: "They are afraid of John." I asked if anyone had heard of the Windy Cove Presbyterian Church (it was built in the mid 1700s) in what is now Millboro Springs. "Yes," they all replied. They knew of the church, but they had not heard of Millboro Springs. This made sense because in their time the area around the mill was called Old Millboro. When the train came through and the railroad station was built, the hub of activity had moved from the mill area to around the railroad station.

When Constance's mother was mentioned, it brought a hearty chuckle from Honey and giggles from Liz. Honey said: "Crazy!! She was crazy. Her name is Eva or Ava, something like that. They say she is crazy." Asked about Ava's house burning down, Honey said: "They say she did it, after he died. Ava went to live with Constance." Liz piped up: "That would be punishment enough for any sin, having to live with Constance." Ignoring the interruption, Honey continued: "They were pretty high class. Their name was Waverly or something like that." Liz said later: "There is a Waverly street or avenue in Millboro." Today the streets in Millboro have all been changed to numbers instead of names, but the main street leading into the nearby town of Staunton is Waverly Road. Both Liz and Honey described Ava exactly as Becky and Constance had. Becky added: "Ava was sad. Her husband had somebody else. He had several women and she knew about all of them."

Suspecting that perhaps Becky's penchant for affairs may have been triggered by infidelity on John's part, she was asked if there was a woman in John's life. A tear seeped out from under one closed eye, and she shook her head in assent: "She's a fancy lady, dresses up in a red dress and black hat with a red feather." Further investigation proved that the woman's name was Rose, and she ran the bawdy house on the edge of town. Becky had not believed that such a thing was possible, and she firmly stated so to Ava, when that demented woman told her of her husband's perfidy. One day, shortly thereafter, Ava picked Becky up in her carriage and drove her out to the whorehouse. Ava had full knowledge of its whereabouts as she had tracked her own husband there on several occasions. As they pulled into the deep, U-shaped driveway, Becky could see in through the windows and opened front door. There was her beloved John standing next to Rose: "He was kissing her on the neck, just like he kisses me."

When the affair between John and Rose was mentioned to Honey, Liz, and Becky, Honey immediately volunteered: "I've seen John and Rose at my boarding house many times. She didn't work out of there—I would not have allowed it—she used to come there to meet John." This knowledge triggered real tears from Becky, who said, sobbing: "I didn't know anything about them meeting in town, too." Becky said she never confronted John about his affair with Rose and that John never questioned her about her activities. Did this change how Becky felt about John—did she love him less? "No, I love him more. John is my heart; Peter is my soul."

Because they were all getting depressed, the subject of Beulah Blackbottom was reintroduced to cheer them up. All three perked up and Honey exclaimed: "Waddles!" That broke their mood and set everyone laughing at yet another name for old Lydia. Honey continued: "I saw her waddle up the street." Becky added: "She drinks, too!"

The discussion then turned to the Top Woods when I asked why Becky and Constance went there. Liz laughed and said: "The reason they went there is because they didn't want anybody to see them smoking." Honey claimed that Becky was trying to get Constance to smoke. Becky said indignantly: "Constance tries to get me to smoke. She smoked before I did!" Liz piped up: "Constance did a lot of things before Becky did. She taught Becky a lot of bad habits!" Honey said: "She didn't teach Becky one thing. She didn't teach her to meet Charley." Liz retorted: "Becky needed him," defending Becky's relationship with Charley in view of John's dalliance with Rose. Liz added that she and John were not on the best of terms because he was fooling around with Rose. She said: "I told him he was a fool and was going to hurt a lot of people with his actions."

To lighten the atmosphere once again, the subject of fashion was raised, and it was asked if anyone dressed up much. Honey exclaimed: "I do!! I have a hoop skirt, but I only wear it for special occasions. It has a high neck blouse with a grey skirt. The dressmaker, Mrs. Tuttle, made it." Becky said: "I don't have a hoop skirt. I really want one, but I have a pretty petticoat." Liz said: "I have a hoop skirt too, and there is one for Becky in the back room. I'm making it. The hoops run up and down. They go from the waist out, all the way down and around. The hoop stuff is made out of a bonelike material. The skirt is cut in panels with a stiffening along each seam. It's easier to sit down in than the other type. It's going to be pretty." I asked how one does sit down in them and Honey explained: "They kind of fold up. You hold the front of your dress down and the back kind of spreads out."

Looking at the town as it was then, they stated that it ran about three blocks. They saw the bank, Honey's boarding house, and the corral. Honey said: "I see the apothecary, the saddlery shop, and Mrs. Tuttle's shop." Then I instructed them to come forward to the present time and see if they could tell me what was there then and is still there now. Honey said: "The barber shop is there in the same place, but different. My boarding house is gone and they've built something else, a general store, but it's all different inside." Although Honey said that she thought her boarding house had been torn down, she was wrong. It was the first thing we discovered when Maureen, Joe, and I visited Millboro for the first time.


## ELIZABETH

On the advice of several people, it was decided to involve another hypnotist in this project for a while, to see if it affected the results in any way. The person chosen was Dee Hahn, a professional hypnotist living in Sun City, about ten miles east of Lake Elsinore.

*"ELIZABETH"*

*Diana Lovegren, born and educated in Los Angeles.*
*Worked in Lake Elsinore City Hall for several years.*
*Has lived in Lake Elsinore for one year; previously lived in*
*Corona (sixteen miles north of Elsinore) for fourteen years.*
*Married to Don Lovegren for twelve years;*
*has three children from a previous marriage.*

He did the initial regression of several people, the first one of whom
was Diana Lovegren.

Diana was something of a virgin to this investigation. By that
I mean she had not heard or read anything about it. She was referred
to me by Jan Dunwoody, who turned out to be another character in
this story and who claimed to see Diana back in Millboro. When
Diana was regressed to an earlier lifetime during the American Civil
War, she was a young girl, maybe six or seven years old. She and
another little girl (who we discovered later was her cousin Lila)

*DEE HAHN*

*Born in Santa Ana, CA, 1938. Received college degrees in*
*California and Kansas; served as medic psychiatric technician*
*in U.S. Air Force. Has been ordained minister for*
*twenty-five years and actively worked in hypnosis for five years.*
*Has lived in Sun City near Lake Elsinore for two years.*
*Has never been to Virginia.*

were walking out in the woods. They had gone there to peek at the Indians. She said, "I peeked at them and they are peeking at me. An Indian is peeking at me!" She and Lila had sneaked out to look at the Indians, strictly against parental orders. The girls were so surprised and perhaps dismayed to find the Indians studying them back that they ran all the way back to town.

The little girl's house was on the edge of town. She said: "There is a railroad in town near the water tower. There's mountains and a railroad tunnel around in the back of the mountain." She could not make out the name on the face of the tunnel, and when asked to do so, she stated hesitantly: "I am afraid of that tunnel. I don't want to stand in front of the tunnel and look at the letters above it. When the train comes, it's loud and the ground shakes. It scares me."

Describing the town: "It's all dirt streets. There's many horses and soldiers, but they keep to themselves. There's material and supplies all around the town. The supplies are going through the town. It's dangerous; I think it's guns and stuff. They're going to have a war with all that stuff; they are all going to kill each other. I don't trust the town. It's trouble; I keep away."

She knew the man who trained horses and she declared: "He wears a black hat. I don't like him—he's mean. The horses are mean, too. He's going to get hurt. He dresses too fancy; he thinks he's a cowboy because of that hat. He's not a real cowboy. Now the sheriff dresses right, because he belongs there."

We were unable to find a name for this young girl during that first regression with Dee. The second hypnotic session with Diana was conducted by myself, and she went back to a party she was attending: "I am dancing and have on a pretty dress with ribbon. The church is where we have the parties, but the dance is in the barn. It is a celebration with lots of food and a fire, lots of kids. I know everybody and am having a good time. We are dancing around the fire. They put something in the fire—a fur coat? It's a piece of cloth, like a figure stuffed with straw with the coat around it." It seems it was our old friend Guy Fawkes again.

Asked about the town of Millboro, she said: "I see a general store. It is near the railroad station and the post office is at one end of town. The boarding house is a big white thing with a rail. There's stores up and down the street on both sides. It's a wide dirt street. I see railroad tracks that go in to the tunnel." When asked if she could see the corral, she exclaimed with passion: "Oh that guy!!" The description given by this child of the town at that time proved to be uncannily accurate, not only as ascertained from other witnesses in the story, but as shown in old photographs of Millboro that were later uncovered.

Directed to the time of the Civil War, she could see the soldiers in town: "They just keep to themselves, back there with the freight, the stuff the horses pull. Everywhere! They put the supplies everywhere! Stuff is piled up in boxes all over town and toward the tunnel. They unload it and more supplies keep coming in. Some supplies go out in the wagons, and sometimes the boxes drop and break. There are lots of people; it's a busy town. It makes me nervous because it's not quiet anymore." Toward the end of the war she was aware of fighting off in the valley: "I see fires and smoke. I knew it! Yes, there's going to be fighting in this town. Everybody's mad! I just want to get out of here!"

Taken back to her younger years, she said she saw a lady with dark hair parted in the middle and fixed nice. The lady was overweight, had green eyes and puffy cheeks. She said the woman looked too old to be her mother and was most likely her grand-mother. There was also a small child with her, a boy who had not been walking long. She was aware of other, older children but could not see them clearly.

Asked if she knew Becky, she answered that Becky had been married to the constable and then added that her father dressed like the sheriff. Excited at having possibly located one of Becky's children, I recited the names of the children to her and she imme-diately claimed Elizabeth to be her name. (Later when conscious, Diana said that she had thought of that name in the first regression, but because her mother today is named Elizabeth, it had confused her.)

Diana Lovegren had never met Maureen or Luke Gremling, who regressed back to baby Peter, another of Becky's children, prior to the time they were assembled together to be hypnotized, but one could sense an almost instant rapport between the three of them when they met—almost as if they had known each other for a long time and were old friends. Baby Peter was approximately three months old, and young Elizabeth was around six when the conversation started. Elizabeth announced: "I did not attend school. I stayed home with my mother and the baby; he's real cute. They won't let me hold him." Becky jumped in and explained: "She's too little to hold him. Priscilla holds him sometimes, but she is twelve. She also changes his pants and helps sometimes. John does not help at all. I have to do the most because the baby always wants to eat—he never seems to get enough." Elizabeth proceeded to name her brothers and sisters: "Priscilla is the oldest; she's twelve. Robert is ten. Rachael is younger; she's around seven." Elizabeth seemed to be the eccentric of the family and she admitted: "I was by myself, a loner."

According to Elizabeth and Becky, baby Peter, who was now about a year old and still nursing, also sometimes ate solid foods: "He eats some mushy things, like oatmeal and mashed peas. He has two top teeth." Describing what they use for diapers, Elizabeth explained: "We have cotton nappies [a British term for diapers that neither Maureen nor Diana would ever use today] that tie at the waist, and he has baggy little pants that my mother made for him. He wears a nice heavy shirt on top. His shoes are little slippers of leather, mostly to keep him warm. He stands, but he doesn't walk yet."

The usual family routine consisted of getting up at 5:00 a.m., or as soon as the sun came up. Becky said: "Sometimes John gets up earlier." Elizabeth added: "We don't wash right away or comb our hair. The pump is outside, and we all have to haul water into the house in buckets." They took turns using the outhouse, which Becky called "the water closet or water shed." Elizabeth said, "It just has one hole so we don't have to share it with anybody."

The school building was made mostly of wood with a brick cellar, and, according to Becky, "There is a bell on top that the teacher rings so the kids who live far away know when it's time for school. Then she rings the bell with the big wooden handle on it to bring the kids in from outside." At some point it was discovered that Elizabeth apparently didn't attend school. When asked why Elizabeth didn't go to school, Becky immediately pointed out firmly and defensively: "Well, she's not dumb. She gets sad if she has to go; it upsets her emotionally to have to go to school." "There's other people there," said Elizabeth in her matter-of-fact voice. "She likes to be alone," added baby Peter. Elizabeth explained: "My mommy lets me watch the other children and that makes me happy. I don't have to join them; I can just watch." Becky added, seemingly undisturbed: "She just likes to be home. I teach her at home." Robert went to school only sporadically, when he was not spending time with grandma Liz. Priscilla was studying to be a teacher, so she attended consistently and took it seriously. Elizabeth said: "Sometimes I walk with the kids up to the edge of the school property, then I run back home."

According to Elizabeth, her cousin Lila was "almost the only one I go anywhere with. We went to the fields and peeked at the Indians." Becky immediately came to attention and announced in a loud voice: "They're not supposed to go there—they'll get whopped!" Whenever anyone got out of line, Becky "whopped" them with her hand. Becky explained that Lila was Elizabeth's cousin and that her father, Jeff, was John's younger cousin. Jeff worked at one time in the general store, but now he was working in the mill and also helped John as a deputy when he was needed. Jeff spent time, a good deal of time, at Becky and John's house and Lila frequently accompanied him. Jeff's wife gossiped a lot, rather like Constance, and Peter complained: "She always got her face stuck in mine!" Lila also played with Peter's face, squeezing and pinching it, much to Peter's disgust. "She picks me up; she's not allowed to, but she does it anyway. She wants to pretend I'm a doll." Becky added: "Lila doesn't have any babies at home to play with." Peter admitted: "I'm used to being fussed over, with all those other kids and mother. Grandma Liz spends a lot of time fiddling with me whenever she is here."

Accidentally addressing her as "Liz," I asked Elizabeth what she would like to do when she grew up, and Becky immediately corrected the record with: "She's Elizabeth!" Elizabeth answered: "I just want to be like my mother, get married, and have a whole bunch of kids." When asked if she and Peter had ever watched their mother make cheese, the two youngsters responded in unison: "Butter, she makes lots of butter!" Becky said primly: "It's very healthy for their hair."

John was gone most of the time and Elizabeth said: "My mother does everything. She is very calm and easygoing; she never complains." Peter added in a quiet voice: "Not at night. Before she goes to bed she cries a lot. She has me in there, and she just holds me and cries. Our parents fight but not much, just words. They fight about dad not being home. He is always gone."

When baby Peter was shown a picture of Charley, he instantly recognized him: "He's a friend of my mom's. He holds me on the horse and lets me ride. Mom doesn't like him doing that too much." Elizabeth announced indignantly: "I don't like it either and I tell mother." Then there followed a truly typical sibling squabble. Peter said: "Elizabeth doesn't like the horses; she's just a tattletale." Elizabeth, shaking her head from side to side, proclaimed: "If that man touches the baby, I go tell mom and she comes and checks! He doesn't have control of those horses at all, so he shouldn't put the baby on them. Every time he does, I tell." In trance, Becky was patting Elizabeth's hand and Peter spouted: "She's just a tattletale. She tells every time I do something wrong and everything anybody else does, too. We don't do much wrong, but she always tells, anyway." Elizabeth, very deliberately: "That's so I will be sure that my mother watches, so that he doesn't get hurt." Peter, from across the bed, stated: "She runs into the house and in a high screeching voice, yells 'Mommy'!!" At this point Becky broke in and tried to make peace: "Elizabeth gets riled up. The other kids don't care like she does." Elizabeth echoed: "They don't care like I do." Becky admitted that she did not like Peter being put up on the horses, but that the baby certainly enjoyed it. Peter explained that his mom was worried that he was too young and that he might fall off or the horse might start running, and he would get hurt.

## LILA

Jan Dunwoody became involved in this investigation in an interesting fashion. After reading some articles about this story in a local paper, Jan, who is an old friend of mine, called to say she might be a part of it. She went on to explain: "Joe Nazarowski (Charley) has his office down the street from me. I took one look at him, and I just felt this hatred—and I don't even know the man! I've never met him, never even talked to him!" Since their offices were close, Jan had encountered Joe on more than one occasion, and the same emotions came up every time. This baffled her until

*"LILA"*

*Jan Dunwoody, born in Gilroy, CA.*
*Married since 1956; mother of two.*
*Has been to Virginia once, the town of Reston near*
*Washington, DC. Had never heard of Millboro*
*prior to this study.*

she read the articles in the paper and it occurred to her that the reason for this mysterious, but very real, feeling might lie in these regressions.

Under hypnosis Jan gave her name as Lila, and when asked the name of the town she lived in, she said: "Wellborn comes to mind." As mentioned earlier, it is very common for people under hypnosis to get letters and numbers confused. In this case Lila had turned the "M" into a "W" and confused a couple of the vowels. Lila said: "I have lived in town a long time. There is a small post office made of wood. The countryside is hilly with lots of trees and the autumn leaves are beautiful."

Regressed to around the time of the Civil War, she said: "I'm standing in the middle of the street in town by myself. I am a woman in my twenties. There is a man in town, Robert. He is a carpenter, and we are planning to marry in six months." When Lila was a teen, her father hired Robert to do some repairs on the farm and that was how she had met him. Further probing disclosed that Lila's Robert was not John and Becky's son, Robert.

Lila thought she was an only child, and after deciding to rename the town Millboro, she said: "I grew up in town, went to school only through the lower grades. When mother would take me to the mercantile, I would hide behind her skirt. I was afraid." It was clear why she and Elizabeth hit if off so well. Lila added: "The mill is going now and they are cutting wood. There is nothing interesting in town that I wish to talk about."

As a teenager Lila described her style of dress: "I am wearing a white blouse and long funny looking pants that come to my calves with a skirt over them. The pants do not show. I wear them when I ride horses." The pants, of a heavy fabric, were designed to protect her legs while riding horseback.

Looking back at her younger years, she recalled: "I think there is a war going on; it's not close, however. The North and South are fighting and I'm on the side of the South. There are soldiers in town; it's their home base. Millboro is a very small town with a railroad station in the middle. The railroad ends here, and they turn the engine around out of town on a turnaround. I see a mountain with a tunnel through it; the tunnel is before they turn the train around. There are a lot of wagons in town carrying bales of something covered up that came off the train."

When she looked down the main street in town, she said she could see the corral where Charley worked: "I know Charley, but I don't like him. He's hateful and mean to the horses and he whips them. He sells horses to the army. He's got bad legs—he walks funny, with a limp. He's just nasty to everybody, miserable, and he likes to drink."

When Constance's name was mentioned, about the only thing she had to say was that Constance laughed a lot; however, she described Constance's house as "the one with the peaks." She thought Constance's husband worked around town, maybe at the bank and that her father owned a business connected with hardware supplies. Asked about Ava, she said Constance's mother "looks crazy! She runs in and out of doors and thinks somebody is after her. However, she is very attractive." Lila remembered Ava's house burning: "A big house was burning. They brought horses and wagons and were fighting with buckets. It's not doing much good though. The trees around the house caught fire too. The weather was cold; it was winter. I see Ava running from the house through the woods. She burned the house because she was mad at her husband, even though he was dead then. The house burnt right down to the ground."

## WHITE BEAR

By far the strangest and saddest story to come out of these regressions was that of "White Bear."

One day a little boy was found standing next to a huge wagon wheel and a couple of deep muddy ruts in the road, just outside of Robin's Nest. He was frightened, hungry, alone, and he was crying. Some Indian children, who were playing nearby, noticed him and because of his unusual appearance—he was white with flaming red hair and a lot of freckles—began taunting him and throwing things. Singing Bird, hearing the commotion, went to investigate and upon discovering the small white child, rescued him from his tormentors. Shooing the Indian children away, she headed the little red-headed boy toward Millboro and told him to walk on into town. Her idea was that if he got down the hill among the whites, he might be taken care of, possibly finding a home.

During Dave Gremling's first regression he seemed terribly confused regarding his life in Millboro and his surroundings. All he could see was a dirt road with trees on either side and open land.

*"WHITE BEAR"*

*Dave Gremling, born in Mansfield, OH, 1948.*
*Moved to Garden Grove, CA, at age eight.*
*Served in U.S. Army in Vietnam.*
*Has lived in Lake Elsinore for twelve years.*
*Never been to Virginia.*

He gave his age as five or younger and added that he didn't have a home. In many of these regressions it was noticed that Barbara Roberts, in the person of Liz or Singing Bird, had a soothing helpful effect on others, and her psychic abilities were very useful, so she was regressed with Dave, and an amazing, appalling story unfolded.

The little boy that Singing Bird sent into town had been on a wagon of settlers heading west or north. There were actually two wagons in the party; one of the wagons had to stop because of a broken wheel. When it resumed the journey, this young boy was left behind to fend for himself the best he could. He cried: "They don't want me, can't feed me—too many people to feed!"

Asked about the wagon wheel, he said: "I see shadows of people. Not my mother; I think it's my mother's sister. They put me off the wagon and said somebody would find me. There were other children in the wagons." He recalled that he slept "under some steps on the outside of a large building. There were rooms upstairs and a storeroom downstairs. I had no food, was very cold, and it rained all night." He continued: "I slept there for several nights, then one night when I returned I saw the door open so I went in, and there was food there. After that, whenever it rained, the door would be open and there would be food inside. First I thought I was stealing, but after it happened several times, I knew someone was giving me food."

Somehow the child survived, and when he was about six or seven, he saw himself living in the basement of the saloon. He said: "It was my job it sweep it out, polish the spittoons and generally keep it clean." In exchange for these services the owner allowed him to sleep in the basement and occasionally gave him food. The child was always hungry and dirty. He kept repeating: "I don't know who I am! I can't find my parents." When asked about school, he said: "Just kids with parents go to school."

He worked and lived in the saloon until he was about seven. Little Eagle knew about the young boy living in the saloon, and one day he asked him if he would like to try living in the woods, out near Robin's Nest. Together the boy and Little Eagle (who the boy always knew as White Eagle) dug out a cave in the side of a mountain, about a mile or so from Robin's Nest, high up in the hills. Little Eagle gave him the name of "White Bear" because he was white and lived in a cave like a bear.

White Bear and Little Eagle became good friends. Little Eagle taught the boy how to survive in the woods. He taught White Bear to use a slingshot with such accuracy that he could bring down a rabbit on a dead run and to find the special rocks that were best to use in the sling. White Bear did have some fire "to cook with." He was only allowed to kill small animals because to kill more than he could eat would be wasteful. However, in the wintertime, Little Eagle would bring him a whole deer because it would keep in the snow. He showed the boy how to keep the deer covered with big rocks so that other animals wouldn't get it and to only cut off bits as he needed them. He also taught him to fish. Little Eagle said: "This is our mountain. This is our home."

White Bear, in his solitary cave, remained suspended between two worlds. He recalled Little Eagle telling him: "Stay away from the Indians. When the Indians come around, jump around and make funny noises so they will think you are crazy. I have already told them that you are. They will leave you alone, give you a wide berth, and you will always be able to stay here. Don't go into their village, but you can stay outside of it, watch them, learn from them, and nobody will bother you." From his cave, White Bear could see hills and many pine and large oak trees. He said: "It was beautiful. In the winter months I lived in the snow. The cave was in the side of a hill, situated in a small canyon with cliffs on all sides. In front there was a clearing of about thirty feet and then a thick forest that rolled down the hillside. One time I followed White Eagle home; it was a mile at the most. The hill went down to a clearing and that's where the Indians lived. I asked White Eagle how he could stand to live in a house. He said he couldn't and didn't."

The stars were White Bear's only family and friends, other than Little Eagle, who came to visit him and then was gone again. He would sit for hours looking at the thousands of stars in the clear air, talking to them, trying to ease his overwhelming loneliness. Occasionally Little Eagle would come by with another boy, a little bit older than White Bear. The two boys got on very well together and sometimes they played tag with Little Eagle joining in the game. White Bear said: "I never knew the other boy's name; White Eagle just called us 'the boys.' He looked like he was part Indian, looked a little bit like White Eagle." Of course this was John. One day after playing together, White Bear wanted to go home with Little Eagle and the boy, but Little Eagle said no, because it would affiliate John with the Indians and they could not risk that.

Little Eagle also came to the cave with home-baked bread in a cloth bag, White Bear recalled: "The loaves were about seven inches long and rounded. White Eagle would bring three or four at a time.

One time he brought me a half a dozen or so, explaining that he was going to be gone for a while. The times he was going to be gone, he brought out beef jerky, candy, and sweet rolls." Also in the bag, he added, "was a stew that was delicious."

The food that Little Eagle brought to White Bear had all come from Liz, who was famous for her delicious crusty loaves of bread. In the hypnosis session it was a very touching moment when a strange look came over White Bear's face as he realized he was sitting next to the woman who had fed him all those years. He said: "Thank you; I never knew who fixed food." Liz, suddenly realizing exactly who White Bear was, exclaimed: "That's the boy Little Eagle took food to the dugout for!" White Bear added: "You make me clothes, too," and Liz agreed: "Yes." White Bear, with an expression of great happiness on his face, elaborated: "White Eagle bring me bread many times! It was good!" Trying to make sure I had the facts straight, I said: "So you were not an Indian—you just lived with the help of the Indians," and White Bear firmly corrected: "With the help of 'a' Indian." This was the first actual meeting of White Bear and Liz, more than 125 years after their lives had so strangely and fleetingly touched.

I questioned whether anyone else in town knew about White Bear, and Liz said: "I don't know; Little Eagle just told me about him. We always called him 'Boy.' I felt like I knew him because Little Eagle would talk to me about him. I never did meet him." Together they laughed over a pair of pants that she had made him, probably out of some old drapery or curtain material—it was flowered and of a heavy, rough finish. White Bear said: "They were more like an old flour bag. I was so embarrassed. I couldn't believe I was really supposed to wear those awful pants. They were so short that they came about one half way up my leg and were held up with either a piece of white rope or a leather thong." Then he added: "White Eagle my friend. He help me, teach many things—to feed myself. Don't have to live in bar no more. Good man!" Liz added: "Strong heart," and White Bear agreed: "Very strong!"

Later when we discussed White Bear's situation, Liz explained: "It was not that unusual at that time for people to abandon their children. Normally, someone would have taken him in immediately, but the fact that there were so many children dropped off like that, people couldn't afford to keep taking them in, so the people in town learned to just turn their backs on them. For some reason, Little Eagle looked upon it as an exchange. His Indian son was being made into a white man, so he would take a white man's son and make him into an Indian."

White Bear grew to be a big, ruggedly powerful man. Not exceptionally tall, but extremely muscular. When he was probably in his late teens to early twenties, Little Eagle took him to meet Daniel, the owner of the blacksmith shop outside of Millboro. White Bear described it as being near a large stream or waterfall, which means that it was probably near Millboro Springs. Daniel was a friend of Little Eagle's and was glad to give White Bear a job. White Bear said: "I can see myself pumping the bellows." He enjoyed the work in the smithy's shop, saying that it cleared his head. Once Daniel asked White Bear to stay with him in town at his house, an invitation that was accepted. However, this arrangement lasted less than one night. Daniel had provided a feather bed for him to sleep in, and White Bear described what happened: "When I got into the bed, I kept sinking and sinking down deeper and deeper. I felt as if the bed was trying to swallow me up! I had to get out of there, quick. How could anybody sleep in something that was going to eat them alive? I stayed in the smithy's house part of one night, then went back to my cave under the stars."

White Bear said: "Smithy called me Derrick and said it meant leader of men. He also gave me a horse." White Bear spent a lot of time exploring the hills outside of Millboro on his horse, and sometimes he would stumble on one of the many stills that dotted the hills around the town. He said: "They make whiskey; sometimes I steal it. When I drink it, I don't have to think."

White Bear was not only isolated from both Indian and white cultures, but he never even came close to experiencing the love of a woman. Asked if he had ever loved a woman, he said: "She don't know." Pinned down as to who the woman was, he replied: "No talk!" It was suspected that it might have been Becky, because she had mentioned earlier that she thought White Bear had done some work for her. Quizzed if he had ever worked for Becky, he smiled and said: "Yeah, I make cow well. Nice lady. She no pay; she no have to pay." He described her as "not tall, had long hair, and lots of kids around." Wondering about something he had said, I asked innocently: "What is a cow well?" Both he and Liz cracked up laughing, and White Bear responded: "I make sick cow well. I give it right food and leaves." Little Eagle had taught him herbal medicine. They both kept laughing over the "cow well" misunderstanding, and White Bear kept repeating, under his breath, "cow well." He said: "Sometimes they brought sick horses to the smithy's, lame, to be shoed, and I would make them well by rubbing leaves on the lame leg. Certain types of leaves that come from my mountain, from a large tree. Sometimes I smash them and make a poultice." Very few people knew that he was so adept at healing.

White Bear was a loner and kept very much to himself. Wherever he was, when things became tense or he felt crowded, he would just retreat to his mountain. When questioned about the war, he volunteered: "It's not my war! Crazy! White man kill white man!"

# INJUSTICE
## by Evie Rieder

What are you waiting for child?
Why don't you give up?
We can tell by the look on your face
that your tears are coming,
quick and clean
to cleanse the human race.
Are you waiting for the cloud
to fall from the sky?
Are you waiting for the earth
to crumble and die?
Are you waiting for the sun
to be blown by the wind?
To circle the universe
and return again?

Is it joy that you feel,
but I feel perhaps not.
I feel it's an anger deep and hot.
An anger that's burning your stomach in half,
To fall to the ground in pieces and rot.
The pieces of you will rot away
and no power on earth can make them stay.
A speck of ash and then you're gone,
back to the place where you belong.

Men will sit on nights so cold
and tell of the stories you once told.
And even with your soul bouncing near,
no man will know that you were here.
It's useless child, but don't give up.
For your thoughts were recorded in time
and years from now in a distant land,
a man will say,
"Those thoughts are like mine."

# THE ETERNAL GARDEN
## by Maureen Williamson

I saw the garden near in bloom
    with promises of old,
when underneath a starry sky
    you took my hand to hold.

I saw the garden fill with light
    reflections come at last
when you reached out to offer
    fragile roses of the past.

I saw the garden bloom with life
    suspended there in time,
a time awaiting rise from sleep
    the night your hand reached mine.

I saw the garden long forgot,
    reborn and made anew
as you breathed life inside of me
    and I breathed life in you.

I'd known the garden long before,
    then knew it once again
when hearts of fire touched together
    hearts of mortal men.

I saw the garden now in bloom
    and saw the roses climb,
when I took you and finally knew
    that you were always mine.

I see the garden bursting through
    in promise of the bond
as we go forth in unity
    forever and beyond.

# CHAPTER THREE

# THE PLOT THICKENS

## SAMUEL

SMOKEY WILLIAMSON WAS LED INTO THIS INQUIRY by Maureen. She had no idea where he fit in, but she was absolutely certain that he was there, in Millboro, somewhere. He told us his name was Samuel in our first regression encounter with him, and he was very agitated, claiming: "I am running and they are shooting at me!" He said: "I live in the south. I'm being chased by men in grey uniforms, but they do not catch me. I was a civilian, a sympathizer. I ran ammunition and sold guns."

Samuel was a printer and journalist from Roanoke. He was married, had two children and was also a very active Union spy, running and selling guns that he had stashed in the cellar of his print shop. Even though he was originally of Yankee stock, he was at odds with the North's cause before the war broke out. He said: "I was very upset and angry with the North at the time, and I got to talking to some people. John was one of them. They set me straight and convinced me that the North was right. I printed a weekly newspaper, *The Pen and Quill.* I had written something about the North, and I had posted it outside; that was right before the war. I got in a little bit of trouble with some of the stuff I wrote. I was threatened, but I had to continue blasting the North to protect my cover."

*"SAMUEL"*

*Ralph "Smokey" Williamson, born in Sicily, 1938.*
*Family moved to San Francisco in 1939 and*
*to the Philippines when he was a teenager.*
*Currently employed by Riverside County Fire Dept.;*
*has lived in Lake Elsinore twenty-eight years.*
*Father of seven children. Had never been to Virginia*
*prior to this study.*

As a journalist, Samuel could travel all over the South with impunity. He went to Millboro (which he insisted should be pronounced "Marlboro," correcting my pronunciation several times) on a regular basis to meet with John. Samuel was regressed early in the study, and he was the one who blithely revealed that John was head of the extensive Union spy ring centered in Millboro, to the amazement of all present. We had not suspected this.

Samuel said: "The spy group meeting place was an abandoned shack next to the stable on the edge of town. The shack was real close to a Confederate outpost, and it made me very nervous. I rode into the corral; people were used to seeing me there because I would interview the high-ranking officers there, presumably to get stories. The townspeople and soldiers were used to me being around." When in town he ate and slept in the shack.

There were several men in the Union spy ring headquartered in Millboro: "Sometimes we would all meet in the shack together. We were all excited. The men came in from many other areas, and at times, several of us would sleep there on the floor. I passed information to John, who passed it on to the Union. One of the men was called Chase; he was kind of a rotund person with rosy cheeks. He came quite a distance to attend the meetings, and he always had a joke or funny story to tell. Another was Mr. Loughlin, a tall, string bean of a fellow, whose cover was also that of reporter on the conditions of the war."

Samuel kept a very low profile around town and went about his business most quietly. He was never seen with John or any of the other members of the spy ring, and he rarely stayed in town more than one night. While the shack looked very decrepit on the outside, inside it was really quite comfortable and well stocked with food and liquor. A young black boy named Coffee lived there, and whenever any members of the spy ring appeared, he would immediately run off to fetch John.

Samuel described Millboro as a very pretty town with a quiet, quaint atmosphere and tall, stately trees. However, it became a mess during the war when the supplies backed up all over town along with the overabundance of soldiers everywhere. Later all the refugees from the valley below camped on every available inch of ground, and the quiet was shattered by the wagons incessantly pulling in and out of town, with the teamsters yelling at the horses and the wagons groaning under their loads.

Jake Bauer was a ne'r-do-well and a drifter. He was a nasty, surly, unpleasant man with a constant chip on his shoulder. Jake wandered in and out of Millboro, doing odd jobs and stealing anything he could get his hands on. In between times he hung around in the local saloon, getting drunk and even nastier. His first serious clash with John came when Jake lowered the fence rails on the property of John and Becky's neighbor, Mr. Phaelan, in order to seize the sheep and cattle that wandered through the open fence. As soon as the livestock strayed out onto the road, Jake would grab them and take them off to sell. Jake was as stupid as he was mean, and after siphoning off a few sheep and cows, he attempted to peddle them right in the middle of town. It took John no time at all to discover that the rustled livestock belonged to his neighbor. He immediately found Jake and at first tried to talk him into giving them back. According to Becky, Jake just kept saying: "Finders keepers—they got out!" Becky added: "When John went to arrest Jake, they had a fight. John finally arrested Jake, but when Mr. Phaelan got all his stock back, he said to let Jake out of jail. After that Jake used to go by John's office and just look at him to make John mad, and he'd look at me, too." This all resulted in bad blood between Jake and John.

A short while after this first run-in, John encountered Jake again, this time outside the post office. Jake made a few disparaging remarks about Becky, and John retaliated by hitting him. Now John was about six feet tall, but Jake was a giant of a man, standing about six feet four inches, barrel-chested with long apelike arms, swarthy skinned; his eyes and hair were jet black. He dressed in dark clothing, and nearly everyone in the story referred to him as dirty and unkempt. John and Jake got into a full-fledged fight in the middle of the street, and quite soon it was easy to see that John was getting the worst of it—Jake simply outsized him. Becky was across the street, in the general store, buying some broadcloth, when the fight started. Coming out of the store, she saw what was happening, grabbed the nearest thing at hand—an empty liniment bottle some-one had left on a nearby bench—ran across the street and clobbered Jake on the head, breaking the bottle. His head bleeding profusely, Jake turned and fled down the street. Becky recalled the fight: "Jake was a big man and was on top of John when I hit him on the back of the neck with the bottle. The bottle broke and Jake started bleeding. He moved off John and John hit him a couple of times. John was so mad, he told me 'You go home and stay there.'"

A few months after this incident, Charley and Jake, who both spent quite a bit of time in the saloon, had a similar encounter.

Somehow Jake had learned, or suspected, of Charley's affair with Becky, and he made some distinctly unflattering remarks about it to Charley and anyone else within earshot. Charley recalled: "Jake was shooting his mouth off about his trials and errors with the ladies. Every once in a while he would throw Becky's name in—he was trying to claim that he had slept with her." Charley finished his drink, told Jake he was a liar, then merely picked up the nearest available chair and broke it smartly over Jake's head, knocking him cold. Then, with the aid of a couple of onlookers, he dragged the large, limp form out of the bar, into the street, and left him there. Jake was not very popular in Millboro.

Samuel had a lot to say regarding Jake Bauer. He described Jake, as others in the study had, as an extremely large man with black hair, a sallow complexion, and a droopy mustache who wore a black hat and kept his pants tucked into tall boots—a generally dirty man. He described how Jake had gotten into trouble with Mr. Phaelan for stealing his horses, but that somehow Jake always managed to get out of trouble as fast as he got into it. Samuel said: "Jake had a big mouth, very boisterous, very pompous. He was a bully." On one of his early forays into town Samuel encountered Jake and they also tangled. Samuel stood up to Jake and earned Jake's respect. He didn't think Jake was used to having people stand up to him. Samuel drank a lot, and he and Jake sometimes drank together. Samuel was probably the closest thing Jake had to a friend in Millboro.

Samuel revealed that while Jake secretly professed to being a sympathizer, he also did odd jobs for the Confederacy when approached and in fact was probably for hire by anyone who had the money.

During one of his earlier trips to Millboro, perhaps even prior to the war, Samuel met Becky. He travelled on horseback and was watering his horse by a stream one sunny afternoon when Becky came wandering by, strolling leisurely through the forest, admiring the beautiful fall leaves. They struck up a conversation. She told him her name was Becky, but he misunderstood her and thought she said her name was Vicky, so he always referred to her as Vicky or Victoria. Becky found herself fascinated by Samuel, and soon a torrid romance was underway. Occasionally he met her at Constance's house, entering through the rear. Becky let him believe that it was her house, but he soon discovered otherwise. He said: "She thought I was a country bumpkin. She put on airs for me, thought she was sophisticated."

First he claimed he didn't know she was married to John, but later became quite evasive when asked the same question. He never told Becky what he was really doing in Millboro, but she guessed— she knew he was meeting with John. Later he heard that she'd had a little boy and suspected that it was his child. Becky admitted later that baby Peter was indeed the offspring of Samuel—his light-colored hair and eyes set him apart from all the other children—and she said John took one look at the baby and knew immediately the child was not his.

John spent a great deal of time at the bawdy house with Rose. Being the center of the Union spy ring in Millboro, he had been ordered by the Union to consort with her in order to obtain information. Constance, Becky's close friend, wasted no time in telling Becky of John's unfaithfulness. Becky already had her suspicions because John had been neglecting his family lately and was never home. This was one of the reasons the affair between Becky and Charley evolved. Charley was a lonely man, and Becky was hurt by John's defection and feeling unfulfilled. One of the girls who worked at Rose's commented: "It was like a three ring circus— John, Becky, Constance, and even Charley sometimes. A busy three ring circus."

Liz bemoaned the fact that John had defiled the teachings that his father had given him. It was explained to her that John thought he was doing the right thing by being a Union spy. We had known from the beginning that Rose was involved in the spy ring, and evidently her girls, whether knowingly or not, were her accomplices.

Throughout the war, Honey and Philip kept in contact by sending letters to each other through John, which helps explain Honey's close tie to John. Evidently, Honey was in a peripheral area of John's spy ring. According to Liz, this is why Rose and John periodically trysted at Honey's boarding house. Honey had a small room on the third floor that she kept available for John and Rose. Before they came, Honey would hide her letters to Philip under the mattress of the bed. When John and Rose left the room, John would take her letters and replace them with letters from Philip to her and any other information that was to be sent out. Then when the courier contact from the North arrived, Honey would put him in the same small room that John used with the messages hidden for him to pick up. That way no one was ever seen passing paper back and forth, and the danger of detection was virtually nil. Honey had an impeccable reputation in town and was the last person anyone would ever suspect of being involved in these transactions.

One evening early in 1865, Becky overheard a conversation in her kitchen between John and a middle-aged man, affluent looking and well dressed in a tailored suit. Presumably, he lived somewhere in the north and was John's contact with Union intelligence. Both men were aware that Charley was a Southern fanatic. Becky heard John say: "Charley has a girlfriend; you'd better check her out." John had no idea that the girlfriend of Charley was his own wife. Becky, to camouflage the affair, had hinted that it was Constance who was involved with Charley. But the Union man had been in the bar at the time of Charley's fight with Jake and had heard the remarks that Jake made about Becky. He knew who the girlfriend was. The wife of the central figure in Millboro's Union spy ring was having an affair with a rabid Confederate sympathizer. It was a situation that was extremely dangerous to the Union cause, but it was Becky who was in the gravest danger. Although John had no idea at the time, the words he spoke were to seal her fate. Becky was bound to know something of what John was doing, and the possibility of her inadvertently relaying anything she knew to Charley was too risky. The Union man knew, at that moment, that for the sake of the cause, Becky had to die.

## CHAPTER FOUR

---

# TRAGEDY

---

IT WAS A WIDELY KNOWN FACT that Jake Bauer was available to anyone, to do anything, for a price. In light of the recurring unpleasantness Jake had encountered with John, Charley, and Becky, it probably took very little persuasion on anyone's part to get Jake to eliminate Becky.

As mentioned earlier, people undergoing hypnotic regression tend to go most often to either a very emotional time in the past life or a traumatic death. In Becky's case it was in only the second session and seemed to come almost out of the blue. Becky was talking about her wonderful early sex life with John, laughing over her mother's dour advice to just lie there and then go wash. I commented that she had a happy life and that Becky was an attractive young girl. Despite the fact that she had five children, she was still desirable. Firmly she stated: "Eight children." Asked how old she was, she answered: "Thirty-six when Jake came." Since I had not heard this name before, I asked who was Jake. "Jake Bauer," she said darkly. "Who's Jake Bauer?" Flatly she said: "He killed me."

When people encounter something terrible or traumatic in a past life, I try to remove them a step from it, instructing them that they are going to see it as if they were viewing a movie or television show. Some people are more able to deal with these things than others. It's important to sense how well someone is handling what they are experiencing. Maureen was quite matter-of-fact at first. When asked about Jake Bauer, she started talking about the incident when he rustled the stock out of her neighbor's pasture. As she got close to talking about the day of her death, her voice started getting shaky, and I suggested she remove herself, observe, and talk about Becky in the third person.

Around January 20, 1865, Becky was in the back yard, hanging up clothes. She described the approach of Jake, her voice hard with anger: "Jake rode up on someone else's horse. Elizabeth and Rachael were in the house. Baby Peter was in the yard with Becky; he was playing with her skirt. She saw Jake Bauer coming. He got off the horse and tied it up. He said: 'This is a lovely day Mrs. Ashford.' She said: 'Yes, it is' and continued to hang up clothes. He said: 'It's a lovely day Mrs. Ashford, to take a walk.' She said nothing; by that time she was afraid. She was afraid as soon as she saw him. He took her arm and said: 'We have to go for a walk.' He forced her into the barn; baby Peter was standing by the door. She tried very hard to be brave because the baby was there." In trance Maureen was getting very upset: "Becky was very scared. Jake wanted her to be as scared as she could be. He told her she was going to die. He said: 'You're going to die today. Look at that baby; you're not going to see him ever again. And John, you're not going to see John anymore. He's not here and he can't help you.'" Jake tore Becky's clothes away, raped her, and then strangled her to death. In trance Becky exclaimed: "There's blood coming out of her ears; it hurts. Why is there blood coming out of her ears?" When she came out of the trance, the idea of the blood coming out of her ears still bothered her. It was explained that as she was strangled, most likely blood vessels in her head had ruptured, thus explaining the blood coming from her ears.

Becky said later that Jake had never bothered to hide the fact that he was attracted to her and wanted her. She said: "He didn't stand a chance with me. I found him repulsive!" Her determined rejection of him no doubt fueled his lust for raping and killing her.

John discovered Becky's body lying on the barn floor. Baby Peter was lying on Becky's still, half-naked body, trying to nurse.

After lifting the baby off his mother, John picked Becky up, covered her, and carried her into their house. He sent one of the children to get Mrs. Phaelan and laid Becky on their bed. Lying down beside her, he cradled her limp form in his arms and cried.

Using her somewhat unorthodox method of reasoning, Becky decided that the murder had been entirely her fault. She said: "I knew because my hair was down. John wanted me to make sure I kept it up all the time, but I didn't want to keep it up. I liked it down; it felt nice." Later she added: "John kept drinking whiskey, and I kept trying to tell him that I did it. If I had worn my hair up, it wouldn't have happened, but that's not true either because Jake was an evil man."

John never did realize that it was his liaison with the Union intelligence that had ordered Becky's death, but it took him no time at all to realize it was Jake who had done the deed. Becky said that after the murder, Jake rode into town and went by John's office. "He didn't say anything; he just smiled, and then he left."

Indeed, Jake's stupidity had finally proved his undoing. Not only had he smirked his way past the sheriff's office right after the murder, but he had loitered around town for some time afterward. Charley described how he, John, and another deputy, John's cousin Jeff, had watched as Jake stole a horse out of Charley's corral in the middle of town. Charley described the incident: "He took one of my horses and we waited for him outside of town. We dropped a rope from a tree, and as he was leaving the rope pulled him off the horse. We beat the tar out of him. All three of us beat him, then we shot him, then we hung him. I don't feel good about the death; however, it felt good to shoot him." He went on: "Then we returned to town and spread the word that someone had hung a Union sympathizer on the edge of town." The townspeople, outside of the group in this story, never did know exactly what had happened to Becky. Liz explained: "Some parts of the Ashford (Aushlick) family tried to cover up her death; they claimed it was due to the epidemic."

# CHAPTER FIVE

## THE AFTERMATH

UNTIL BECKY'S DEATH THERE HAD NEVER BEEN a rape or murder in Millboro. The entire area was totally shocked and traumatized beyond description by this brutal incident. This became increasingly obvious as we talked to more and more people who were drawn into the story.

During her first hypnosis session, Liz was directed to the time of Becky's death. It was immediately evident that this had been a mistake as there was a vehement abreaction. First she gasped for breath, then hyperventilated so intensely it became necessary to instantly arouse her from the trance.

Mary, Liz's old neighbor and friend, had returned to Millboro a few months after Becky's murder. She claimed that Liz was absolutely beyond grief, and she did everything in her power to comfort the woman. Liz was literally unable to function for months after Becky's death. Mary said: "I wasn't sure she was going to survive." Constance withdrew for weeks after Becky was killed, was unable to talk, and found it difficult to deal with the tragedy. According to Ava, Constance never did fully recover from the shock of Becky's death. When Constance, in trance, was placed anywhere near the time of the murder, she became ice cold and shook uncontrollably. Once I asked Constance to look at the graveyard where Becky was buried, she replied: "I won't go there. I don't want to see Becky's grave. I don't want Becky to be dead."

Later, Constance said that Becky was buried just outside of town, in a family plot. It was not in the direction of Warm Springs but the other way. This coincides with what others have said and appears to be correct. Constance stated several times that she always felt that Becky's affair with Charley had resulted in her death, but she never knew why. It was much later that we discovered how true Constance's feelings were.

When Honey was instructed to go to the time of Becky's death, she became very upset and could scarcely talk: "Somebody killed her. She was outside her house in like a shed, and he put something around her neck. Charley cried; he was very upset. Everybody in town was upset. I am hugging him [Charley]. He was in love with Becky. Nobody knew they were having an affair. I knew though, because I saw them." When Millie was returned to the conscious state later, she said that she could feel Charley's head on her shoulder for a long time afterward. After Becky died, she had just held him and rocked him while he cried on her shoulder for hours. She added: "I have seen the man who strangled Becky. He has got black clothes on and a black hat; he is dirty. He comes and goes. I heard his name, Jake Bauer. Everybody's scared; they don't know who did it. Later I heard that somebody killed the man who murdered Becky."

Evidently, Samuel was not aware of what happened to Becky because he claimed that several times after the war he had returned to Millboro in an attempt to see her. When he eventually learned of her murder, it upset him badly.

John was absolutely devastated by Becky's death, and for a long time he just cried, completely debilitated. He began drinking constantly. Charley and others covered for him many times in his work. He was completely unable to come to terms with what happened or to resume anything resembling a normal life. Everywhere he looked and everything he saw in Millboro reminded him of Becky. Every time he looked at his children, he was forced to face his own involvement in her death.

Asked if John ever got his life straightened around, Honey said: "I don't think that he ever did." Liz said: "He would not bring the kids to me; he was upset with me because I didn't think he was treating Becky right." When Liz was asked if she thought John had brought this all upon himself, she just started to cry.

The townspeople never really knew the reason behind Becky's death. Because they were embarrassed by Becky's sordid reputation and the sensationalism of the death, the Aushlicks (Ailstock's) went to great effort to cover it up.

During the session with Becky, Elizabeth, and baby Peter, it was discovered that something very terrible had happened to little Elizabeth. Unknown to anyone, Elizabeth had not been taking a nap when her mother was killed, as previously thought, but had snuggled up in one of her favorite hiding places, the hayloft of the barn. Becky was brought out of the trance, but she remained lying on the bed between baby Peter and Elizabeth. Elizabeth told us: "I was in the barn when they came in. I heard him dragging her. I heard a noise and they were there. I didn't know what to do; mother was fighting hard and I thought she would win. The baby was about two. It all went so fast, then mom was quiet. I stayed where I was, in shock. I was there when my father found her. I couldn't believe that she was dead." Asked if she saw the man that killed her mother, she first said: "Jack," then changed it to "Jake."

Elizabeth was very frightened and remained quiet, staying hidden in the barn for a long time after it happened. She had wanted desperately to get out of there but was too afraid. Her mother lay there not moving, and Elizabeth knew she was badly hurt. Still, she remained hidden, frozen to the spot with fear until eventually her father found Becky, took her into the house, and sent one of the children to fetch a neighbor. Through all of this Elizabeth, in a state of shock, remained hidden in the barn. Much later, when she did return to the house, she saw her mother laid out on the table.

It is not known whether at this point Elizabeth told her father what she had seen, but that would provide one explanation for why John, Jeff, and Charley were able to know so certainly who murdered Becky and position themselves to capture and execute Jake. Or perhaps Jake's smirking slink past the sheriff's office immediately after the murder told the whole story.

While Maureen was conscious and Elizabeth and baby Peter were in trance, there was so much she wanted to ask them, she said she didn't know where to start. She asked if the older kids had thought she had abandoned them and Elizabeth answered: "Oh, they all knew." Were they embarrassed in the community? Peter said: "Rachael was, so was Priscilla—that's why she left." Elizabeth said that Becky had a bad name in town "because that red-haired lady, Constance, talked a lot."

They both agreed that much of Becky's bad reputation was the fault of Constance. Peter said: "She would just put her nose into everybody's business and she'd lie and gossip." Becky commented that she would like to hear what Constance had to say after she was killed, and Peter complied: "She said that you were a whore and that you tried to get her to act the same way." We asked if they had ever heard Constance talking to their father, and again Peter answered: "Yeah, papa slapped her!" Surprised, Becky said: "Really?" Peter explained: "He was a very peaceful man, too. Constance was talking about mom, and she was really starting to get on dad's nerves, so he just slapped her and told her to leave. They were on the street in the middle of town. It was about a year after mother died, right before I went to live with Honey." Elizabeth wanted to know why Charley implied that mother told some secrets. She said: "I overheard him say something about mom telling some secrets, or maybe the man who killed her thought she did."

The question was raised if very many people knew how their mother had died. Elizabeth answered: "They spread the word that she had died in the epidemic. Why should we tell people the disgrace of what that man did to her? They covered up a lot because of her dignity."

At this point it was explained to them that their father was a Northern spy and that Charley was a Confederate spy. Jake had been hired to kill Becky by people who thought she was a threat to the cause. They suddenly realized that Charley and John both had a hand in their mother's death. Peter said: "That's why! Oh my God! I thought it was just because the man who killed her wanted to disgrace her." It was quite a moment of revelation. Roughly 125 years later, Peter and Elizabeth finally understood why their mother had died.

Becky was buried on a little hillside right outside of Millboro. Elizabeth said it was not really a cemetery as she could not see very many other graves there, but it was a nice place, pleasant and very private. It had been John's idea to place her there. As a tender token, John had buried Becky's favorite little mirror with her. He and the children had gone to the gravesite later and placed small rocks all around her grave to delineate it, with one large rock for a headstone. As a final gesture they placed a wooden cross at the head of the grave, with a little inscription on it. Elizabeth could only make out the words "Wife and Mother."

The children were cared for by various people in town. John finally took baby Peter to Honey and asked her to take care of him. Honey said: "I didn't adopt the baby; I just kept him. He didn't have a place to go and I was real fond of him. He liked me too and looked at me like a grandma. He was my little Sugar Pie, just my little Sugar Pie."

Charley had a very difficult time accepting Becky's death. It became clear the more we delved into the investigation that he had never realized or accepted how much he really loved Becky until after she was gone. When the war came to an end, he left Millboro as soon as possible, a totally bitter and frustrated man. He had lost the only two things in life he held dear, Becky and the cause of the South. He never married, and after leaving Millboro he worked as a lawman in some areas, busted broncs, and repaired fences. There were renegade bands from the Union Army called Union Jacks roaming the south, looting, raping, pillaging, and burning. One of the things Charley did was use his old links to the Confederacy to help maintain order in some of the towns. Gradually he worked his way to Georgia where he set up an active underground movement that went on for a long time. He called the Yankees "Yellow Bluebellies" and was familiar with all the sayings of the times, especially: "Save your Confederate money boys, the South will rise again!"

In Georgia he again trained horses, and the Union went out of their way to contract with him for their horses, one of the reasons being, according to Charley, "so that they could keep an eye on me." They watched him closely but never did realize that he was meeting with his people every night in the saloons. He was organizing them to rise again and directing them in acts of sabotage.

Charley died at a relatively young age. He was rabble rousing one evening in his favorite bar and got into a fight—he loved to fight when drunk and meanness took control. He caught a man cheating at cards and the fight was on. When he left the bar, there were a couple of men waiting for him, and he said: "I got beat up pretty fair!" After the fight he made his way to his shack on the outskirts of town, where he died in his sleep from a head wound sustained in the fight.

Charley left no family and no friends. He died a lonely and broken man. While in Millboro, he had loved Becky and even felt close to her children. He took baby Peter to his corral so he could watch the horses, and one time, because Becky worried about Elizabeth feeling lonely and left out, he carved Elizabeth a small wooden horse, which she cherished for years. When White Bear and Liz were in trance together, I had asked White Bear if he ever loved a woman. He said: "She don't know." Later, when taken to the day of Becky's death, he turned toward Liz and instructed loudly: "No talk!" When Jake Bauer was mentioned in conjunction with Becky's murder, White Bear commanded: "Don't talk!!" He was telling the hypnotist he would not discuss it and commanding Liz not to talk either. Maureen had suggested earlier that we quiz him regarding the murder, because she felt as though he had been there, somewhere. White Bear stated that he had not wished to discuss Becky's death or Jake Bauer, and he did not want Liz to talk about them either. He had mentally communicated this message to Liz, and she laughingly admitted that she got his message very clearly.

In the conscious state, Dave Gremling realized that White Bear thought he could have prevented Becky's murder. He had been in the forest moments before and had seen Jake going up the road to

John and Becky's house. When he heard that she was murdered, he was overcome with remorse because he felt he could have done something to stop it. He had been, he admitted, very much in love with Becky: "Sometimes I would ride by her house through the woods and catch a glance at her, but I never approached the house. She didn't like me and I knew it. The only time I went up to the house was when I was caring for the sick cow, and then I went there three days in a row. She didn't ask me to fix the cow, but I had heard it was sick, giving bad milk, and I knew I could help. I think she was afraid of me, probably because the Indians had spread it around that I was crazy. While I was fixing the cow she kept a wide berth—she was obviously afraid of me. I was secretly in love with her, but in that life I never had any type of relationship with a woman." He continued: "Jake came riding by on a large horse. If I had just gone by and said 'Hi' to him, he would have known someone was in the area, and he probably wouldn't have killed her. I blame myself for her death because I could have stopped it. I was built like an ox."

## BABY PETER

The mother of two boys, Maureen said that her oldest son did not figure in this study, but she knew that Luke, the younger boy, definitely did. He was baby Peter, the blond-haired, blue-eyed boy she had borne of Samuel. Dee Hahn did the first regression with Luke Gremling.

When taken back to the approximate time period, Luke said, "My name is Peter and I'm about nineteen years old. I'm on my way to Texas to be a Texas Ranger." He said he was about forty miles from the Texas border, had built a fire, and was getting ready to sleep.

Then he was instructed to go back to roughly one year of age: "Mom's hanging the laundry on the rope. She is very pretty. She's got long hair that looks like gold when the sun shines on it. My father has dark hair and is tall and handsome. I have some sisters,

*"BABY PETER"*

*Luke Gremling, youngest son of Maureen and Dave Gremling.*
*Born in 1973 in Orange, CA.*
*Has lived in Lake Elsinore since age of one.*
*Has never been to Virginia.*

but no brothers. Mom is Becky; my dad is John. I never did really know my father that well as he was never home much; he was always down at the office. He is the constable. I want to be like him." Peter added: "I see the barn and the house; there are lots of trees around. Mom usually is around the house, cooking and doing the laundry."

As experienced previously, he regressed to the most traumatic time in his babyhood, to his mother's murder: "There is a man coming toward the house on his horse. I have seen him before, but

I don't know who he is. He is wearing black clothes. He doesn't look very happy. Mom is not very happy to see him. Guess she doesn't want him to come over because she is telling him to stay away, but he is coming over and getting off his horse. I don't know why, but he's trying to hurt my mom!"

Dee instructed Peter to move forward in time, at this point, to the age of four: "I am with Honey sitting at home. We're always happy now. I live with Honey because my mother is dead. Mama's with God, the best place to be." Shortly after Honey had lost her baby to the fever, John had asked her to take baby Peter to live with her, and the baby filled the void left by the loss of her two children. Peter continued: "I have always been happy with Honey. She is playing the piano; she plays good, the song called, 'When the Rebs Come Marching Home.' It's about the war. Why do people fight?" According to Peter: "Honey's husband is gone, at work or some-where." Actually, Honey's husband was dead. He went on: "I don't know where my dad is. I don't see him very much. Grandma Liz comes over often; she's here now, in the kitchen making lunch. Honey sings good. Right now she is singing about a one-legged lady with a one-legged dog. It's a funny song. I don't see my sisters very much—they say I'm too young to do anything important."

He continued: "I live in Virginia. I don't know the name of the town. It's a nice house, white with yellow trim and a nice porch, green grass in the front, and roses. Sometimes I can hear the train, but I don't like it; the sound bothers me. I have never seen it and don't know where it is, but it's loud."

After his mother died, baby Peter had moved in with Honey, but not for quite a long while. He said: "It seemed like a long time because papa was always there and he was always crying. I was sick after my mother died. I never did feel good. Don't know why I was sick; I just was. I missed my mama. I was sick because my mommy wasn't there. My stomach was upset and I threw up a lot. I was like that for a long time. Finally they gave me something that was sort of off-white in color. I don't know what it was, but it sure tasted good. I think they got it from the goat because they always gave it to me when they came in from seeing the goat."

He said: "Grandma Liz and Honey are always joking around with each other, and they talk about how I'm growing like a weed. For lunch we had meat pie with lots of meat, vegetables, and gravy, also some ice cream and juice. We always had fun when Grandma and Honey were together. Honey talks kind of slow and funny. I try, but I can't copy her. She talks the way some of the people who come into town talk." When we asked about his last name, he said: "I can't pronounce it. Whenever Honey says it I think of ashes. I don't know how to spell it."

At age ten, Peter recalled a party he attended at school: "Everybody from school is there, ducking for apples." With a mischievous smile on his face he added: "I stick my head in for the longest time and get real wet." He explained that if Honey were there, she would stop him. For some reason she was terrified of water and would never let him near it, except to wash and bathe. At that time he was unaware that her oldest daughter had drowned.

After bobbing for apples, he was sitting at his desk eating the fruit: "I am talking to Becky. She has the same name as my mom's and I like her a lot. I am having fun today; it's just so much fun being with all my friends. Honey should be here soon to get me; she usually comes and gets me from school." Peter was having such a good time that he didn't want to come back to the present time and said so several times as Dee was counting him up.

In the conscious state, an embarrassed Luke refused to tell us Honey's pet name for him. Finally, after much coaxing, he admitted that she called him, in a heavy southern accent, "Sugah Plum" or "Sugah Lips," but most frequently, he was her darlin' "Sugah Pie!"

During his next regression, baby Peter, at the age of about one, was again vague about having an older brother, but he was very aware of his older sisters. He described his sisters as having dark hair and dark eyes and himself as being blond. He reiterated that his father was the constable and worked in town. His mother took him with her wherever she went, but occasionally he was left with an older woman who cared for him when his mother or sisters were unable to.

When presented with a picture of Charley, Peter immediately recognized him: "I have seen him; he is at the house sometimes and once in a while he plays with me. He's a pretty nice guy. He has a place in town and has a lot to do with horses. He holds me on the horses sometimes."

Sometime after the war ended, Philip Taylor, the Union soldier Honey loved so much, came back for her, and they were married. They moved to the Tidewater Plantation in "Cosher" (Crozier) on the James River, northwest of Richmond, where they lived out their lives. Peter was about seven when this move was made. He recalled: "There was a man that went with us; I called him papa because that's what Honey wanted me to call him. He acted like a papa to me and we got along real well." There were other children in the house that they moved to who were all much older than Peter. He did not know if they were Philip's children, perhaps from another marriage, or if they were Philip's nieces and nephews, but sometimes they played with him and they were all very nice.

At around the age of eighteen Peter said: "I was trying to be a Texas Ranger. I'm too young, but I will just lie about my age. I had a girlfriend, Becky, from school. I would like to marry her, but I think that she probably doesn't want to marry me. I never did ask her. Becky and I go to parties together, but Honey doesn't like it; she doesn't like my being away. I go see Becky whenever possible and we go for walks or ride horses a lot." There were other girls around that he liked, but he only saw Becky. She was the only one who mattered to him.

He continued: "Since I graduated from school, when I'm not with Becky, I just hang around and do chores, like carry coal and feed the horses. I live on a big plantation where they grow tobacco. The crop has big, bushy leaves and it doesn't taste very good. Honey doesn't like me to get near it." After the crop was harvested, the big leaves were dried by the few Negroes who were paid to work there. Peter said: "There are houses in back where the slaves used to live. The Negroes that we pay now live there. They are pretty nice." The huts that formerly housed the slaves were made of wood and tin.

As you entered there were beds on both sides of the room, a large wood burning stove used for cooking and heating, and a sink in the corner.

When the subject of his father came up, surprisingly enough, he answered: "My real father is not the constable; he was a printer from Roanoke." This was a fact that no one thought he was aware of. Later when conscious, he explained that there was a little Negro boy in town named "Cocoa" who used to bring money to Honey while they still lived in Millboro, saying: "Here's some money for you from your real daddy." Hearing that others in the group had mentioned a little black boy named Coffee, he said: "Yes, that was his name." This revelation upset Becky—she was unaware that baby Peter had ever known that John was not his real father.

Peter did not see much of his family after going to live with Honey, especially after they moved near Richmond. He said: "I don't go back to Millboro because Honey does not let me travel much, but grandma Liz comes on the train sometimes." Honey indeed kept a tight rein on him and did not like for him to be out of her sight.

After graduating school, Peter worked around the plantation for a while, then took a job on a neighboring plantation. Finally, when he was around eighteen, he said: "I left Virginia and headed for Texas to be a Texas Ranger. Just took my horse and left, did not say goodbye to anyone. Honey didn't know—she would not have let me go. I left her a note. I had my own money from working on the neighbor's plantation." Knowing that if he had announced he was leaving, Honey would have found a dozen different ways to prevent it, he did the only thing he could. He just left.

He went on: "It took two months to make the trip. I worked along the way, stopping in a town and working as a deputy for a while or sometimes working in the saloon, getting rid of the drunks." Upon reaching Texas, he headed for the Mexican border down through Dallas to the San Antonio area. He said: "At first they wouldn't take me there, because I was too young (I told them my real age). So I went to another Ranger station further down and I lied about my age, told them I was twenty-one, and they took me, gave me a colt .45 six shooter and three weeks of training. We went to New Mexico for the training, where there were a lot of high cliffs. We would stand at the bottom of the cliff, about forty or fifty feet away from it's base, and about every hundred feet up there was a target. There were four targets and we had to shoot all four targets in a certain amount of time. When that was done, they would set up more targets. The targets were just a painted piece of wood, swinging from the end of a rope. We had to run, jump, roll over, and then shoot the target, roll over again, and shoot at another target. We did that until the targets were all gone. We were all trained by ourselves, individually—it's better training for a Ranger. Sometimes they would send in just one of us to clean out a whole town. The Texas Rangers were the best. They gave me a gun and gun belt, a brown leather shirt, and denim pants."

Shortly after becoming a Ranger, Peter was stationed in a small town just inside of Texas from the New Mexico border. He had met a girl there named Sally, and in time their friendship developed into love and he thought about marrying her. He explained the reason he had been stationed in that town: "I was put there to watch for a felon who had just been released from jail. He had threatened to go back to that town to kill the mayor because the mayor had put him in jail. I was in the bar, with Sally, getting a drink when I heard some gunfire. I had been drinking and wanted to show off for Sally, how much of a man I was, so I walked out, and there was the released felon, just coming out of the bank. He had shot the mayor, but the mayor wasn't dead, just wounded. Sally was standing by the door of the bar, and as I walked out I shot the felon in the shoulder. The man returned fire and unfortunately he shot Sally. I shot him again and killed him. Sally was dead—he had shot her in the chest. I felt very bad; I had wanted to settle down and marry her."

Peter later did marry, at the age of forty-two: "Her name was Becky (the third Becky in his life), and she was from California." They had met in Arizona while he was there training another Ranger. Because it was felt he was too old to be an effective Ranger, he had been transferred to the training program. Becky was visiting in a small town Peter passed through to get to the training area when he met her, and she decided to come along as an observer. She was impressed with the Ranger training and was equally impressed with Peter. They started seeing a lot of each other, and before long they were married.

He said: "We had three children. I retired from the Rangers and we finally wound up back in Virginia. At first we lived around Marlboro [as he pronounces it]. I went back there to see Honey but she was no longer alive, then I tried to investigate my mother's death. I learned the constable had caught the person that did it and the man had been hung. There wasn't much else to investigate except as to why she had been killed. Some said that it was just because the man loved her and he couldn't have her so he killed her. I heard the story that had been circulated about my mother dying from the epidemic, but that was a bunch of bunk. There were stories to the effect that my mother was a whore, that she took that guy into the barn, teased him, and he killed her. Those were stories that went around earlier, in Honey's time. By the time I went back everyone had pretty well forgotten about my mother. The constable was gone and no one knew where. Grandma Liz was gone too; she died." Peter and his family did not remain in Millboro long. It was too painful for him with all the old, unresolved memories.

We took Peter ahead in time to his death. He said: "I was shot at the age of sixty-four in New Mexico. I wanted to see California and stopped in New Mexico on the way. My kids were there, even though they were grown. We were just passing through, on a trip. One of the men that I had put in jail had been released, and when he saw me, he shot me. I didn't have my guns; I had put them away for good long ago. I was a tourist." All in all, Peter felt he'd had a good life, despite the tragic death of his mother.

In the conscious state, Luke said that Honey was a dear woman, but she smothered him with her love. When he was seventeen, she was still calling him her "Sugar Pie," and he found it very embarrassing. She would never let him go anywhere near water and never allowed him to go on a train or anywhere by himself. His first love, with the first Becky, never had a chance to develop because of

Honey's obsessive jealousy. He finally realized that if he were to have any life of his own, he would just have to leave, unannounced.

## RUTHIE

Maureen introduced me to Jackie Spagnolo. The two had been friends for years, and Maureen stated that Jackie was in the story somewhere, but she did not know what role she held.

Once again we went straight to the Guy Fawkes Day celebration, which must have been the best party of the year in Millboro, judging by how many of the people in the story brought it up. She described the festivities: "There's lots of drinking going on and dancing—everybody is there. The women take heaps of food. There's a big bonfire and a figure stuffed with straw and rags with a face all wrapped up; they are hanging it from a pole." She became upset at this part of the ceremony and said: "It's not nice to do these things. They get too wild; it's terrible." After the hanging the party really got wild and out of control, but she loved the dancing. Her name was Ruthie, and she lived outside of town with people who were not her parents; they were an elderly couple. She did not think that she went to school but was tutored at home.

When the war started, Ruthie left the farm and the couple who had raised her and moved into a place where she wore a red dress and danced on a stage. She did not leave the town, just moved to another house, situated a little distance outside of town. The house, however,was not just any house—it was Rose's bawdy house. She said: "It was a big, barn red house; there were about five or six girls in the house. We got along okay because we had to; we had no choice." She explained that she really did not have a boyfriend, but there were several men in her life and sometimes they paid for her time. Ruthie left the house where she grew up when she started consorting with men. The old couple would not have approved of her lifestyle, she explained: "I went to Rose's because I wanted to get away. The old couple were good to me, but I was all by myself, all alone. I went to Rose to get a job."

*"RUTHIE"*

*Jackie Spagnolo, born in Winchester, VA, 1930;*
*family left Winchester in 1932.*
*Worked for many years at Disneyland in Anaheim, CA;*
*now retired. Has four children.*
*Lived in Elsinore area for twelve years.*
*Does not know if she has ever been to Millboro.*

In the first regression, Ruthie was somewhat coy about her situation. When asked if she was a "fancy lady," she said: "Well, I dress nice and have my hair fixed." When Rose's name was mentioned, Ruthie stated: "She has a lot of girls and they live where I do." Then, she volunteered: "There was one girl that had red hair that Rose didn't like. She didn't work in the house; she lived in town and her family was monied. She had a lot of kids. I think her name was Constance. Rose didn't like her because she was cutting in on Rose's business; she took people away."

Ruthie knew the man who trained horses in town and said: "I saw Becky talking to him a couple of times." Asked about Becky,

*"RUTHIE's" lover, "RUNNING BEAR"*

she said: "I think Becky died. I heard she was killed. Constance was mean to Becky." Ruthie seemed to want to stay on the subject of Constance, and I had to wonder what her preoccupation was—nobody had ever mentioned Constance to her, either in or out of hypnosis. She continued: "Constance told people that there was a romance between the horse man and Becky. You see, she wasn't Becky's friend; she said she was, but she wasn't. She always got Becky into trouble, but Becky kept being her friend. Nobody in town liked Constance, not really."

Constance's mother, Ava, was mentioned and she started laughing and nodded in affirmation. She described Ava and said: "It was the way she would look at you; you just always felt funny when she looked at you. She was different." Laughing, Ruthie explained that she did not want to say anything about Ava's antics because she didn't want to get on the bad side of Constance, which was the wrong side to be on! After some coaxing, however, she did say: "Ava would see things that were not there; she thought people were chasing her and ran away from imaginary things." She added, laughing: "She was quite a character and was so funny at times."

In the second session Ruthie was regressed with Liz. First Ruthie saw herself at age five. She said: "I see a big, black woman taking care of me. There is no mommy around; I'm not able to see my mommy. All I see is the older couple that I stayed with, Uncle Bob and Aunt Emma. I don't know their last name." Liz volunteered that she thought Ruthie was related to Ava. To this Ruthie nodded in agreement and explained that that was how she knew Constance so well. Liz said: "I think she's Ava's niece."

We figured out that Ruthie was younger than Becky and Constance but older than any of their children. No one seemed to know what had happened to Ruthie's mother, although it was agreed that she had died when the girl was very young, possibly even in childbirth. Earlier when we regressed Ava, she had made vague references to there being some other girl in the house, but the only daughter she was aware of was Constance, and she could answer no questions regarding the other girl. Liz and Ruthie decided that Ruthie's mother had been Ava's sister and that because the mother had died when Ruthie was very young, Ava had taken the child in to raise. Ruthie's hatred of Constance had become more pronounced in this session. She said: "She was mean, a snob and supercilious, looked down her nose at me and everybody. Nobody was as good as she was. Constance was secretly jealous when I went to work in Rose's house."

When we probed a little further, it was discovered that as a child, Constance had not wanted to share her domain and raised such a fuss over Ruthie invading her home that Ava had turned the girl over to the older childless couple who were anxious to give Ruthie a home. This also helped to explain Ruthie's deep-seated hatred of Constance. When I asked why Rose disliked Constance, it was Liz who grunted and supplied the answer: "Constance was cutting in on Rose's business! Rose was selling something that Constance was giving away. There was lots of jealousy and resentment there, more than anyone ever knew. I think Constance hated

Rose because of what she was doing to Becky, playing around with John."

How did Ruthie explain where and how she lived to the sweet, proper older couple who had so lovingly raised her? Ruthie grinned and Liz started to giggle. Liz said: "They knew she was there, but they thought she was doing something entirely different, They thought she was the bookkeeper!" Ruthie told us that life in the bawdy house was pretty interesting, and if she had it to do over, she would probably do it again. She said: "It could have been a lot worse. We usually worked with only one man a night, maybe two. I got paid well. There was liquor served downstairs, and if you wanted to dance, you could find a place to dance. I did not drink much, but I really liked dancing." Ruthie mentioned that Jake Bauer came to the bawdy house often and fancied himself quite a lady's man, but she said: "Nobody wanted to be with him; he was dirty, but he kept coming back all the time."

Marriage records from Millboro show that Becky's daughter Elizabeth married John Thacker in 1868, so I asked Ruthie and Liz if they had heard of him, and Ruthie said: "Yes, he was there in town; he was kind of a nuisance." Liz said: "The name is familiar; maybe he married Priscilla. No, she left town after Becky's death, went to Tennessee to teach school." I told her that he had married Elizabeth and asked if either knew what kind of business he was in. Ruthie said: "Maybe he ran the general store," but Liz interrupted to say: "He ran the feed store." Previously both Peter and Elizabeth had agreed that Elizabeth's husband had indeed run the feed store.

Ruthie solved one of the many mysteries of this increasingly interwoven story, how Becky and Ava came to be riding in Ava's carriage to Rose's house. She said: "The reason Ava caught John at the bawdy house was because she had come out there to see me. When Ava saw John, she went back to town, got Becky, and hauled her out there to show her what her husband was up to."

According to others in the study, Ruthie was very pretty and did not lack for suitors, but marriage did not interest her. Ruthie was thirty-two when she died. She was the victim of a random shooting accident, and her death was sudden and quick. Liz could see the incident: "The shooting was not done with malice; it was an accident. I see him, on the ground floor. He's just acting crazy, cutting up. He is drunk, dancing by himself. He pulled his gun and shot through the ceiling. Ruthie happened to be upstairs and the bullet hit her in the stomach. It was early in the evening and she was sitting on a chair, talking to a customer. She died very soon after being shot. It was painful but did not last for long; she lost a lot of blood. The shooter was a young man, very handsome with dark curly hair; he was a stranger to us. There was not a big scandal when it happened—it was the type of thing people expected to happen in a bawdy house."

Jackie today has a great fascination and affinity for American Indians. Asked if she could see any explanation for it back in Millboro, she said: "We had Indians around there," and when the name Robin's Nest was mentioned, she said: "That was where the Indians lived. There was one there that I liked. I met him one day when I was out in the woods; he spoke a little English. He was very nice looking. I called him Running Bear." Liz was smiling and nodding her head. She said: "I know who he is." Ruthie continued: "There was a very big romance there, right from the beginning. I had to sneak around to see him. He wouldn't have dared to come to the bawdy house; he would not have been let in. If the towns-people had known about this affair, they would have been really hard on me. The Indians were treated badly then; they had no status at all. They were nice, very nice people. I liked them." When asked if she had a child by this man, Ruthie refused to answer, although later she said that there had been a baby: "A little girl; the Indians kept her. I went out to see her periodically. They were nice, very loving Indians. They would like to have been accepted by society but knew that they never would." Ruthie added: "It was about seven or eight years after the Civil War when the Indians were run out of Robin's Nest. It was before I was killed." The relationship with Running Bear was always kept secret, but deep in her heart, Ruthie knew that it was right. She loved him desperately and said she always felt clean and wholesome with him.

When Jackie came out of trance she was flabbergasted. Years ago, she explained: "I was taking an art class; we were talking about painting Indians and Indian relics. The teacher had a bunch of pictures of Indians, and when I saw this one picture I said: this is my man. I felt so close to this Indian when I painted him. He was so easy to paint; it flowed." On coming out of the trance she suddenly realized the uncanny resemblance to Running Bear. There, hanging on a wall in her home for years, had been the picture she had painted, a portrait of Running Bear.

In closing, Ruthie made an interesting observation about the town of Millboro: "I noticed that nobody back there ever talked about their past or background, where you came from or what you had done in life. It was because Millboro then was the Siberia of Virginia. A lot of people in town were there dodging the law or creditors or wives, etc." Millboro was, and still is, geographically isolated and quite inaccessible. Also, it was located on a somewhat remote spur of the Central Virginia Railroad, making it even more desirable to anyone who might be running or hiding.

## SHARON

Sharon Olive is related to Millie Sproule (Honey) and lives in El Paso, Texas. When she heard about my study from Millie, she was so certain she was in it somewhere that she flew in from Texas to be regressed. We were never able to get a name for her, so we will call her Sharon, her name today.

When regressed to the middle of the Civil War, Sharon said: "I see a big white house with pillars out in front. A road circles around the house. Somebody is coming out of the house, an older black woman; nanny comes to mind. She is real happy and bright. I feel like I am part of the family, but no one is around; the place seems to be deserted. I don't understand the war. I hate it—both sides will lose. I am in the south, in Virginia. The house is on a small hill with lots of subtle green rolling hills. Nearby there is a

*"SHARON"*

*Sharon Olive, born in Mankato, MN, in 1943;*
*currently living in El Paso, TX. Divorced, has two children*
*and one grandchild. Has never been to Virginia or*
*heard of Millboro until this study.*

creek, but we get our water from a well. There is no one here to
tend the land. I have a garden with vegetables, for the family, and
I sell some to the neighbors." Sharon seldom got into town, but she
did know that there was a railroad there and many soldiers coming
and going. At the time, Sharon was about thirty-five or forty years
old. She said she lived in the house with "a white-haired old man
with a bad back and legs. He dresses nice but not fancy. He is good
to me and very, very happy that I am here with him. I don't know
exactly why I am here, except that it was decided that it would be
a much safer place for me to be."

Explaining that, at the time we were talking, she was walking around outside the house, she described a large, solid, heavy wooden door. She said: "It leads to the basement. There's a large rock on either side of the door; there are old wooden stairs going down. There's something about the basement! There is some activity in the basement. There are people down there! Men!"

Asked to tell us about the men in the basement, she said, "They are captured or lost Union soldiers. The old man and I help them get back to the Union lines. The house is very well set up for this—there is a large, well-hidden tunnel that leads out of the house. That's the way the men get into and out of the basement." She explained: "Sometimes people, who had heard stories that we were helping the Union soldiers, would come to the house and make some excuse to go into the basement. The old man and I would make a lot of noise going down the stairs, and by the time we got down there, all the soldiers would be hidden in the tunnel."

She added that this effort had something to do with the railroad in Millboro, but it is possible that she was referring to the Underground Railroad movement, as such operations were called then. Obviously the owner of the house had been assisting Negro slaves escape to the North through the tunnel for a long time prior to the Civil War. Sharon explained: "We lived in terror every day that we could be caught and executed." John, the sheriff, was about the only person from town that she knew: "John visits occasionally; he was in league with the old man." John also brought whatever food he could salvage for the men hidden in the basement.

After the war was finally over, she said: "The soldiers were burning a lot of leftover supplies and accidentally burned down a barn in the process. I can see lots of black, billowing smoke. Most of the blacks came back after the war; they felt it was their home. They had left to join the Northern Army with the blessing of their owner, the old white-haired man. There were many people around; soldiers were returning along with the former slaves. I see rows of small wooden sheds out in back where the blacks live."

Although Sharon rarely went to town, she said: "I see a church in town, white with a large steeple." It was probably the one near the cemetery that later burned down. She also mentioned "the ubiquitous wagons pulling out of town all day and night. They raised an awful dust."

Later we realized that this house where Sharon lived was the same house in which Honey had attended the dance and fallen in love with Philip. It was also the same house that Ruthie lived in, with the older couple, before the war. Probably the one compelling reason that Ruthie desperately wanted out was the illegal activities occurring in the basement, first slaves being run through to freedom and later Union soldiers being smuggled back to their lines. In 1850 the Fugitive Slave law was passed, imposing stiff penalties on anyone caught harboring or assisting a runaway slave. A Southerner caught hiding Union soldiers during the war would have been shot for treason. Poor Ruthie probably left her home with the older couple from fear of being executed for treason, only to be randomly and needlessly shot in the whorehouse.

## THE FAMILY GROUP
### Honey, Liz, Becky, Elizabeth, and baby Peter

In a sort of final roundup of Becky's family, a group hypnosis session was conducted with Honey, Liz, Becky, Elizabeth, and baby Peter.

The subject was raised of how settlers passing through an area would sometimes leave their children behind, dropping them off the wagon and continuing on. Liz said: "It's not uncommon at all. These are hard times; children have to be fed. It's a strain on the family." Becky added: "The Negro boys, they sell them and their mothers never know where they are." Evidently it was also a practice, in those times, for unfortunate black children to be stolen from their mothers and sold as slaves.

While we were talking about people passing through the town, the discussion was directed toward the refugees that swarmed over Millboro in the last year of the war. Describing them as pathetic, Elizabeth said: "Some had bandages on their heads." Honey

### THE FAMILY GROUP

*In a state of deep hypnosis, left to right:*
*"ELIZABETH," "BECKY," "HONEY," "BABY PETER,"*
*and "LIZ" (SINGING BIRD)*

claimed: "Some are walking; some are in wagons. They are dirty with stringy hair, just skin and bones. Even the horses are skinny. Liz has a family living with her. They are nice people, but they don't have anything at all. I have fed a lot of them passing through." Becky added: "They have been burned out of their homes, lost everything. They are poor unfortunates."

All were instructed to turn their attention to the big, white house with the pillars out front, the house that was used to smuggle Union soldiers out through the basement. Honey excitedly piped up: "That's where we went dancing!" They all agreed that the house still stands today and that most of it is in pretty good shape, except for the roof, which Elizabeth said, "is a mess!" Liz stated: "It has good floors, beautiful floors." Honey, with a rapturous expression on her face, declared: "That's for dancing!!" Becky concluded: "The orchards are overgrown and the leaves on the trees are all black and brown."

Becky volunteered: "Negroes were being run through that house too; there was a tunnel that led from the basement of the house down to the creek." The contraband Negroes and soldiers had been spirited both in and out of the area on flat-bottomed boats, which would have been much quieter than wagons in the dead of night. When asked if that tunnel was still there today, Liz said: "There's all kinds of stuff, like stone shelves on each side of the passageway." Elizabeth added: "Now the water has eroded it; you can barely see it, but it's by the river." Honey added facetiously: "I don't think they use it anymore."

Later Liz explained that the tunnel had originally been a root cellar that had been expanded, then turned into a tunnel that opened on the bank of a deep, active creek running behind the house. The creek side opening was hidden under the exposed roots of a large tree. Today the creek is dried up; the water has probably been diverted and there are tall, grassy weeds growing in the former creek bed. (Author's note: On a later excursion to Millboro this plantation house was located, exactly as described. I talked to the present owners about the possibility of allowing us to expose the tunnel, but they were not amenable to this proposition.)

Some of the group knew Ruthie and said that she had been looked upon as a black sheep because she chose a whore's life instead of marriage and a family, especially since she was so pretty. The feeling was that she could have married well and led a good life. When asked why Ava did not keep Ruthie and raise her, Honey hissed under her breath: "Because she's nuts!" Becky said: "Because Constance was so jealous." Liz was the only one of the group who knew about Ruthie's affair with Running Bear and of the little girl who resulted from it.

When Honey was shown a picture of Charley, she became very emotional and was unable to speak. Becky explained: "Honey's sad because Charley's life was so tragic." Asked if she ever thought that Charley was a Confederate spy, Honey gave her typical answer: "I keep my mouth shut! There was a lot of talk, but I couldn't say anything."

To lighten the mood, the subject of baby Peter was brought up. He immediately claimed that he was still sick when he went to live with Honey, although not as bad as he had been. Honey said: "He was a good baby; I spoonfed him a little gruel and goat's milk."

Elizabeth chimed in: "She did a good job." Everyone goaded Honey to tell them about the time baby Peter went for a walk by himself. They were all laughing because her obsession to keep him close to her was well known. "He wasn't gone too long," she stated, "because I didn't let him out of my sight that much. I found him down by the railroad track, smacked his rear end, and hauled him home real fast." Honey explained that she had been doing the laundry, turned her back for a minute, and he was out of there: "He just moved too fast!!" According to Peter: "She came running after me, screaming like a banshee!" Honey said: "Yeah, he was just out that door; everybody had to watch him. I felt like putting him on a leash." When Peter protested: "You wouldn't do a thing like that!" she just chuckled.

Everyone agreed that Honey played the piano so all could sing. Peter started with: "A one-legged woman with a one-legged dog." Honey claimed that she made up all those things as she went along. Liz remembered: "A one-legged cat and a one-legged frog," and this stirred Honey to action. Trying to get everyone to sing, she said: "Come on Liz, a one-legged cat and a one-legged frog." Then she turned to Peter and commanded: "Sing Peter!" Shyly he said: "No, it's your turn." Honey countered: "I'm playing the piano—you sing!" Then she continued: "Liz is real good; she's good at making up things." The three agreed that they really had a good time when grandma Liz came to visit. Honey said: "She's a pleasure to be around and a good cook!"

Moving ahead in time to when Peter was about seven years old, Honey told of taking Peter somewhere to see John: "I took him out several times to see John; he used to meet us in different places. Once I took Peter to see him, but John didn't want us there. He was abrupt with us; he had rejoined the Indians by that time." Peter reiterated: "He didn't want us there." Sadly, Liz stated: "It wasn't right—Peter should be able to see his father. I wanted Peter to see him and Peter wanted to see him." Peter recalled: "It was a pretty neat place, though. There were a lot of animals around and people dressed really funny." Honey added: "It was an eerie place; I didn't care for it. Some were dressed in Indian garb, some wore just old clothes. There were a few tepees [Peter explained these were reserved for the tribal elders], and the rest lived in a big, long house, a barracks type of building. A lot of campfires around, a lot of people singing, just weird stuff. The other Indians just ignored us, paid no attention to us at all." As if by way of explaining John's behavior, Liz added: "Peter doesn't have any blood line," meaning that Peter was not John's child.

A can of worms was opened when Elizabeth was asked if she had gone to see Peter in Millboro or Richmond and she answered loudly, in clear, clipped tones: "No, because Honey said not to and I said I wouldn't, as long as she didn't let him ride on a horse because I knew he would get hurt. We made a deal." This touched several of Peter's sorest spots and he erupted: "Tattletale!! I liked riding on the horses! She always went screaming home to mommy. In a high-pitched voice she would scream 'Momm-eee, Mommm-eee'!!" Liz said: "He was gonna get hurt on a horse." Honey, at the same time: "I didn't like horses either!" Peter, muttering: "That's your tough luck—I liked them." Honey: "It was no problem when Elizabeth asked me not to let him ride them because I didn't like them anyway."

When it was suggested that maybe Peter was upset because none of his family came to visit him, all three spoke at once. Elizabeth, forcefully: "Honey didn't want that!" Honey: "It was better that way; it would have upset him." Peter, ranting: "There was a train, you know, a thing called a train!! Some people walk, you have two legs, you have a horse." When asked why she didn't want his family to visit, Honey explained, somewhat tearfully: "I didn't want them to ever take him away from me." Elizabeth summed it up: "Then the new town they moved to would never know that he wasn't hers. She took good care of him."

When the group had calmed down a little, Honey was asked if she knew a printer from Roanoke. She answered: "I know of him, Samuel. He puts out a paper. He brought information about the war." Asked if he was a spy, she said: "They are not supposed to be called a spy, but he let out a lot of information." Next I asked if she knew a black boy named Coffee. Peter chuckled and said he knew him. Honey asked Peter: "Is that the one you were playing with?" Peter said yes, and Honey continued: "His nose was always running. 'So wipe your nose,' I would say. 'Use your sleeve, your sleeve!'" Liz interrupted, saying: "He would come and get John, running into John's house yelling [she mimicked him in a falsetto voice] 'Missa John, Missa John.'" Becky explained to no one in particular: "He couldn't read." Honey admitted that Coffee had brought her money from Samuel from time to time, and Liz revealed that before her death, Coffee had brought money to Becky, also from Samuel. Honey said: "I didn't want the money from Samuel." Someone mentioned that Coffee was responsible for telling Peter that his real daddy was a printer in Roanoke, and Peter declared: "I never liked Coffee after that." Honey: "I didn't want him around and I didn't want the money!!"

There was a brief discussion of whether there were any black "Aushlicks" (Ailstocks) in Millboro, and Becky announced loudly: "There sure were!! Abraham and Absalom. They were brothers; they came in from another area and had a big pile of kids." Honey, laughing, explained: "The Ailstocks tried to keep all of that a secret," adding under her breath, "They would." Liz said: "The Ailstocks, in town, deserved it." Peter retorted: "No they didn't!!" The reason the two free-born mulattos came to Millboro, according to the group, was that they were run out of another county so they followed their white half-brothers to Bath County in the 1830s. When it was suggested that their relatives in Millboro were less than overjoyed to see them, Honey, Liz, and the whole group howled with laughter, and Liz, who thought the Ailstocks were a bunch of snobs anyhow, said: "They deserved it!!"

Carefully, so as not to upset Honey too much, the subject was raised about Peter's departure for Texas. She immediately gasped and said: "Oh my God, he can't do that!" Crying, she continued: "Peter left a note saying he was sorry, but he had to go out on his own and he loved me." In trance, Peter turned to Honey and, trying to comfort her, said: "I had to leave; there was nothing else I could do." Honey said: "I had gone to town with Philip. When we came back, he was gone. I found the note pinned to my pillow; he had planned it." She never got over his leaving and always thought he would come back, but he never did, not as long as she lived. She had Philip, but that didn't make up for her precious baby Peter. She tried to get Philip to go after him and bring him back, but Philip wisely, if futilely, counseled her to let him go, saying: "He's old enough to go. Let him go." Peter to Honey: "In my letter, I said I was going to be coming back." Honey, ignoring him, kept crying: "Philip said he was a man, but he's not. He's all I had." Peter tried again unsuccessfully to comfort her: "I said in my note I would come back," but she continued to grieve her loss, saying: "It didn't matter!"

Elizabeth was asked if she knew John Thacker. Surprised, she asked: "Did I marry him?" and continued: "I was very young, about twelve or thirteen. I wasn't all that crazy about him, but it was the thing to do; he was there and he loved me." Peter said that when he finally returned to Millboro, in his adult years, he had met John Thacker and liked him very much: "He was a real nice guy and he liked guns, too. I showed him mine and he flipped." Elizabeth stated: "He worked in town, in the feed store," as others in the study had concurred. Peter said: "He ended up owning the feed store," and then, still trying to placate Honey, he said: "I came back to see Honey, but she wasn't there." Elizabeth continued: "I had a few children, maybe three. John had money and I had a nice life with him." They had lived for a while in John and Becky's old family house, but then they moved into a newer one, and after standing vacant for a long time, Becky's old house eventually burned down. Peter concluded: "Only the barn didn't burn; it was the only thing that didn't burn. Somebody came and bought the land, tore down the barn, and put up another house." Someone corrected him, saying that a church was erected where Becky's house once stood, and he agreed that, yes, it was a church and it still stands today. John Thacker's name was brought up because there exists today a record of Elizabeth marrying John Thacker in Millboro in 1868. This would have been just three years after Becky's death, and as Elizabeth was about nine when her mother died, she would have been twelve or so when she married in 1868. Elizabeth died quite young, in her forties, after Peter had returned to see her. She described her illness: "Tightness in my chest. I could hardly breathe; I had a fever and a cough." Liz added: "I think it was cholera."

Peter was asked if the other girl, Rachael, had been there when he returned to Millboro, but he said no, Elizabeth was the only member of his family that was still in town. Elizabeth said that Rachael married and moved out of town, had left on the train.

At the end of the hypnosis session, before they were returned to full consciousness, the group was asked if there was anything more anyone wished to discuss, and Elizabeth announced: "I am going to tell you the rest of the song. They were all one-legged, and they all danced around the one-legged stool! Honey would back off the piano and twirl around on the piano stool." Singing, she continued: "We got a one-legged horse and a one-legged cow, one-legged dog." Here she stopped because she didn't know the words, then she continued: "And they all danced around the one-legged bench . . . chair? Then Honey would twirl around on the stool. I don't have my one-legged people right." Peter informed her: "After a one-legged dog, it's a one-legged cow." Elizabeth, singing merrily: "A one-legged dog and a one-legged cow, one-legged man and a one-legged . . . cat, and they all danced around the one-legged stool." Peter added: "They all danced around the one-legged lady with the one-legged dog." Elizabeth: "Then Honey would throw her hands up and spin around on the stool and we'd all laugh." Liz elaborated: "Peter liked that; he liked it when they all threw up their hands and swung around." Peter noted: "After a while she would have to swing around the other way to get the stool back down."

Someone, ill-advisedly, mentioned horses, and Peter immediately charged Honey with: "Why don't you like the horses?" She replied: "I don't want you on them. You're too little to get on those horses." Then Elizabeth jumped in, her voice rising: "You are not supposed to be on those horses, I tell you—you will get hurt! The only reason you didn't die from a horse is because you didn't get on one!" Honey tried to explain to Peter: "See, horses buck and kick," but Peter was not to be deterred and declared defiantly: "I got on them anyway!" Honey retorted: "That's because Charley put you up on there. We fought about that!!" Peter continued that he got onto the horses despite Honey, and she muttered: "And you got your fanny spanked, too!" Becky interrupted: "Charley would hold him on; he was okay when Charley would hold him on."

Elizabeth announced that she went and told whenever this happened. Peter retaliated: "She told on everything!" Elizabeth countered, again: "You should not be on a horse. That's so important; you have to listen to me!!" Liz observed: "Those horses weren't all trained; they were wild," and Honey agreed firmly: "Yes, they were just wild animals." Becky was just too trusting, Liz concluded. Becky answered this by explaining that Elizabeth "told because she was afraid he would get hurt." Peter, all riled up again, said: "She'd go screaming to mommy. She should mind her own business; she's nosy." Becky interrupted the entire scenario to announce: "She's different than the other children." When it was tentatively suggested that perhaps Elizabeth was a trifle weird, Becky angrily exclaimed: "No!" Everyone agreed that Elizabeth was in fact a very sweet child, but definitely a little different. According to Becky, Elizabeth was not only different but special because she saw things that others did not see. It was her contention that Elizabeth, even as a small child, was very psychic.

Peter then turned to Honey and in an accusing tone asked: "How come you didn't like Becky from school either?" Honey informed him that he had been too young for romance. She had not liked Becky; she was definitely not for him. Peter said: "You said that she was dirty. She was always clean." They argued further, then Honey was asked if there was any girl in the school that she would have approved of for Peter. Everyone laughed but Honey, who replied: "Yes, there was, but he was too young." Peter said firmly: "I did not like Mary!! She was a little homebody." Honey answered that as far as she was concerned, "that was what he needed, somebody who would take care of him."

This last exchange finally ended the session, but they all acted like they wished to stay in the trance and continue arguing and chatting. It was as though they really enjoyed the chance to talk together after 130 years.

When conscious, Becky announced that Peter had a very guilty conscience for having left Honey so long ago and that he needed to face it and work it out. Honey laughingly stated that if she had her way back then, she would have kept baby Peter home, unmarried and tied to her apron strings until he was about fifty years old!!

# CHAPTER SIX

## THE EPIDEMIC

### SARAH

LISTENING TO THIS STORY UNFOLDING from my subjects under hypnosis, much of it was sounding familiar to me. Joe Nazarowski, who regressed to Charley, was the first who said: "You, Marge, you were the nurse. You were head of a group of nurses who were sent in by the Union government right after the war to fight the epidemic."

Lila and Elizabeth came up with more details. They said they could see a great deal of smoke in the area coming from the valley below, which was being torched by Sheridan and Custer's troops, and from the town of Millboro: "They are burning the mattresses and blankets; it's from the disease. Anyone who was sick, they burn their stuff, right in the middle of the street, in a big bonfire." At first, prior to the end of the war, they took the sick people to the church and the school, but by the war's end the epidemic had spread so extensively that they quickly ran out of room in which to isolate the ill, and they never were equipped with any trained personnel to treat them.

Help finally arrived in the form of a small group of Northerners from New York, about twenty of them, mostly women who were nurses and a few men who were doctors. Elizabeth pointed her finger at me and stated: "You were there; you got off the train. Some

*114*

*"SARAH"*

*Marge Rieder, author of* Mission to Millboro *and primary hypnotist in the study*

came in a wagon, but most came on the train. You were there with a group of nurses and about five or six doctors." According to Elizabeth, I had blonde hair and light eyes, was very pretty and happy. Lila said: "It was nice; people were happy. They came with medicine and tents. We were so glad to see them. The nurses came in and took charge of this awful epidemic." Elizabeth added: "They were tough—they had to be—but they all smiled. They did a good job, worked all the time."

Throughout this entire hypnosis study, after experiencing strong feelings of familiarity and déjà vu, I decided that I was merely relating in a psychic way to what I was hearing, not an uncommon phenomenon between hypnotist and subject. However, after Joe so adamantly insisted that he saw me in Millboro, I finally decided to be regressed myself. It was interesting that Becky had no knowledge of me throughout this Civil War story, but we must realize that she was dead by the time the medical team came to town.

Enlisting the aid of Dee Hahn, I underwent regression, and my first impression was of being a girl when she was about fifteen. It was a shock to see her curly blonde hair, laughing eyes, and sweet smile because she was a ringer for my oldest sister, Betty, whom I look nothing whatsoever like today. She wore black bootlike shoes that buttoned up over her ankles, a cotton skirt with ruffles, and a pretty blouse. The girl was happy, lighthearted, and had an effervescent type of personality, full of life and vigor. Not particularly concerned with her future, she just wanted to dance and have a good time with her friends. While she was enjoying herself, she was certain that her father was trying to figure out a way to get her married to the best possible candidate. It was obviously uppermost in his mind, if not in hers.

Father was a large, portly man wearing a coat to his waist with tails in the back. He was probably a banker, but whatever he was, he ran things in a nice way, and he loved his young daughter, who was an only child so far as we could determine. My father was easy to see clearly; my mother was more difficult. I finally did see a woman I thought to be my mother. She was slender faced, rather stern and could not understand what I was so happy about all the time. My father and I had a great rapport. He ran things in the house, but he gave me a lot of leeway, let me do things my own way much of the time. He and I were always able to find something to laugh about together.

The year was about 1850 or 1855, far enough before the Civil War so that no one was thinking about it or expecting it at all. We lived in a big home in New England amid heavy, massive furniture and highly waxed hardwood floors. There was a woman in the kitchen wearing a black dress, white apron and cap, obviously a domestic. She is in charge out there in that great big kitchen, walking around doing her chores, putting things in a pan on the stove. She and I were good friends and got along well together, with a lot of mutual respect and love.

It seemed to me that the girl was very bright, but I was unable to ascertain whether she went to school or was tutored. The family was well off and would have been able to educate her in whatever way they chose. We went to church every Sunday, which I didn't much care for. I remember having to get dressed up in a dressy dress, my little bonnet with white gloves, and sit quietly in a big, typical New England steepled church. We did not go to church out of any particularly strong religious feeling; we went to be seen and because everyone in our town went to church on Sunday. The streets in the town were either brick or cobblestone, wide and lined with huge trees that hung over the sidewalks. It was a pretty town of medium size, not too big, not too small.

In regards to my name, at first Beulah or Sybil came to mind, but later Lila said: "Susan?" and immediately the name Sarah popped into my head. It seemed right, and both Lila and Elizabeth agreed that it was. Looking back at that pretty, unfettered girl, it didn't seem that anything in her young life had ever upset her.

Going ahead in time, Sarah was training to be a nurse. She wore a serviceable, long black dress with a high neck and leg-of-mutton sleeves and a white apron pinned to her chest that tied in back. Her hair was pinned up in a prudent bun. She was in a big brick building, probably a hospital, scrubbing floors and doing chores. Sarah was learning a great deal in that building, mostly about how to work, as she had never been required to do any work at home. She was busily running about carrying bedpans and basins, washing things, and tending to patients. The ambiance was stark and bleak—it was not a pretty place—and Sarah was looking forward to getting through her training, an apprentice nurse's training of some sort. Later, when conscious, I realized that Sarah had not gone into nursing as a young girl. She had married, as her father had intended, and had only become a nurse after she was widowed in her late twenties.

Reading a book compiled by John R. Brungardt, *Civil War Nurse: The Diary and Letters of Hannah Ropes* (University of Tennessee Press, Knoxville, 1980), brought several things to light. In the front is a picture of Hannah Ropes. She was a dark-haired, dark-eyed woman with a long slender face. This was definitely the woman I had pictured as Sarah's mother. The feeling perseveres that Sarah's mother was dead and that this woman, Hannah Ropes, became a mother figure to Sarah. In her letters and notes, Ropes makes several references to a nurse named Sarah J. Cashman, "the pretty widow." From what the people in the study have stated and from the flash I got of the young girl Sarah, I know that she was very pretty, an uncommon trait among the female Civil War nurses. Several subjects have remarked that Sarah was extremely efficient and well organized, that she moved quickly and effectively. (This was not always said in a flattering way; some of those slow Southerners resented her because she expected them to move quickly, too.) In her book, Ropes also makes references to Sarah Cashman's efficiency and organizational ability.

Continuing the search, I hypnotized Jan Dunwoody again, back to the life of Lila in Millboro. Asked if she recognized the name Cashman, she answered: "She came in after the war to help with the sickness. She is a Yankee nurse, tall, blonde with light eyes. Her first name is Sarah, Sarah Jean Cashman." Lila and Elizabeth frequently carried food out to the tent hospital. Because they were young, they very probably addressed Sarah as "Miss Cashman" and would be more likely to know her last name than the adults in the study who had called her Sarah. My feelings were strong that Sarah's maiden name was Irish, maybe Callahan or Cassidy.

Moving ahead in time, the war is starting now and the significant thing is the war. None of us really thought it would ever happen; we still don't believe it and we don't like it. There's a lot of ambivalence as to whether we should be fighting. Why not just cut them (the South) loose? we all asked. Sarah did not really know how she felt about it. The thing that appalled her was the bloodshed, the boys who were coming home without arms and legs. It didn't set well with her at all. Even though she was not clear in her own mind exactly what her politics were, she inherently felt that the cause of the North was right.

Sarah's comments were: "Economically if you divide the country, it weakens it, and we don't need a weak nation. I think slavery is abominable. We've got Indian trouble out west; we don't need the Southerners deciding to go their own way. This nation needs to stand together and fight the Indians. There's enough going on in the western part of the country keeping us busy without worrying about those Southerners.''

Going ahead to a further stage of Sarah's nurse's training, she was wearing a grey uniform with an apron pinned to it and a little cap with the edges turned up. I have been elevated now, either graduated or near the end of my training, and feel much better about life. Probably the most significant thing in my life, at that time, was being capped, finishing my training, and the fact that the war had started. My friends are going, and as I said, there are boys starting to come back minus limbs. It's a terribly graphic image of what's going on down there.

Once again moving ahead a little further in time, Sarah became very agitated and upset, crying: "Oh, God, the horror of that war! The terrible mangled bodies, the constant roar of guns. I must be in a field hospital or an aid station. The bodies just keep coming in, those poor kids. God! It's so utterly appalling. How do you ever get used to it, something as horrible as this? Jesus, God, those arms and legs have got to come off; there's no way around it, no way to treat them. Gangrene sets in and they die. We have to saw off the arms and legs of those young men—it's just terrible. God only knows how we deal with it. I don't." When asked how long she had been dealing with it, she answered: "Way too long! It just keeps going on and on; it's endless. I am at the outskirts of the war in the northern part of the Southern fight. I am not far from Washington, near the wilderness, somewhere where they had those terrible battles, maybe Fredricksburg."

Continuing, Sarah recalled: "They are bringing in the dead bodies and those wounded boys, the screaming, the bleeding—it's such a nightmare! I see litters with bodies on them. The wagons are back there; they come in on the wagons from the front lines, drop them off, then go back to pick up more wounded men. Our supplies are coming in slowly and there are some tents there, but mostly we are using the buildings we have commandeered in town, turning them into field hospitals. Fredricksburg comes to mind, somewhere around there. There are so many battles and they move around so much. It is 1862 or 63; now there are no tents, just buildings. We are hauling them in, in litters, on the rugged dirt streets in wagons, then we stash them wherever we can find a place to put them, hopefully up off the floor, out of the mud and the dirt. We need cots to put these kids on; it would be better if we could get them up off the ground. We have nothing much to work with really. The supply wagons come in bringing things the trains have delivered from the north, Baltimore, Philadelphia, Boston . . . I don't know, wherever they can get supplies. They bring blankets, cots, and things we need, but there's never enough. There's not enough medicine. We just put a ropelike tourniquet on those kids and twist it with our hands to stop the bleeding; that's all we can do. We use a tourniquet before we saw a limb off. We try to get them drunk on liquor before we do this, but we're even low on liquor."

Later, Sarah was out of that horrifying battlefield situation and back up north in a hospital somewhere doing administrative work: "We try to stick together, the doctors and nurses, but I don't feel much comfort. I feel like I am alone with this awful mess. There's so much on my shoulders; I was still pretty young when all this started. There's not much laughter, not much joy, but it was better when I got back up north and was working in the hospital; there wasn't the terrible pressure. Right now I get the feeling of being away from the firing line, out of the danger zone and away from battle. It's such a relief! I am wearing a clean uniform and have plenty of food, blankets, cots, and things to work with. I am out of the situation of horror that I was in a couple of years ago. The feeling of terrible frustration is gone. I know it's still going on down there, but I am not in it anymore, at least not for a while."

Finally, the war was over, and Sarah experienced feelings of relief and horror at what it had cost, but the great feeling of relief overshadowed all other feelings. Somewhere along the line, Sarah had met the man that she was going to marry. She was excited and happy at the prospect of getting out of nursing, becoming a married, settled woman again, and getting her life on course. Unfortunately, it didn't work out that way. The war was over, but the South was in a desperate situation. There was a raging epidemic and people were dying by the hundreds. She said: "It's just a disaster; we have got to go down there and help those people fight this epidemic. They asked for volunteers, and old dummy me, I stood up and said, 'I'll go.' We got on a train, five or six doctors and twice as many nurses, headed for Virginia. We didn't know what to expect, and by the time we got through with the indoctrination lectures, we were scared to death!" The group was lectured on how very unpleasant it was likely to be because, after all, they were Yankees going into the southland. They were warned that the people would probably yell obscenities, call them names, throw stones or rocks, and possibly even fire guns at them. The danger and risk were never minimized, and they were informed that if they chose not to go, they could back out. No one did. It was emphasized that they would just have to take whatever abuse was handed them. They must stay in control at all times, retain their dignity and decorum, and not provoke unpleasantness or try to retaliate in any way. They were to go down there quietly and do their best job under what could be very adverse circumstances.

### Arriving in Millboro

When the train pulled into the Millboro station, Sarah and the group of doctors and nurses were terrified. They had all been in battlefield locations during the war, but their work had always been to the rear of the fighting. Now they were about to step right into the line of fire. Sarah cried as she told about the reception at Millboro: "When we got off that train, we were scared to death. I was the first woman off because I was the head of this group of women. The tension was so thick you could have sliced it with a knife. Lila said later, 'We figured you'd come down here and poison us, you know, in the water or something' and we, the medical group, were sure they were going to shoot us one at a time as we stepped off the train." Something happened to break the tension. It concerned a very small girl. Possibly, she stepped forward and offered a single flower to Sarah, and Sarah, overcome with emotion, kneeled down to the adorable child and kissed her. It was as though someone had thrown a switch. The fiddle and harmonica started playing Dixie, and the townspeople were so glad to see them. The men and boys came forward, grabbed their luggage, and others steered the group toward waiting carriages. They were so grateful, it was embarrassing. It was, to them, as if we were heaven-sent.

Mostly it was men who greeted them, but there were a few women dressed in little bonnets and long jackets who remained in their carriages. The townspeople opened their homes to the visiting medical personnel, and as they were on their way to the homes they were to stay in, Sarah said the group was shocked to see the mountains of supplies piled up all over the town. They immediately held a conference with the town officials to decide what needed to be done. There was a local doctor who appeared very qualified and whose opinions they listened to. He explained that it was crucial to get the sick people out by the river. Millboro had been picked as the place to concentrate treatment of the plague victims because there were plenty of open fields and cold water available to fight the fever. The doctor and local officials had already picked out the spot where the treatment center was to be located, and the medical team went immediately to work. Tents were brought in and set up, and the train was commandeered to start rolling in the necessary medicine and equipment. Within a few days the tent city was in operation and patients started coming in droves. Many were brought in by their families, but the majority, arriving by train and wagon, were brought by soldiers in both Confederate and Union uniforms. It was important that the suffering be consolidated in one place because it was clear that whatever the disease, it was contagious.

Sarah was in charge of the nurses and acted as administrative overseer. Trying to keep order was the real problem. It was not the utter chaos of the battlefield aid station, but it was a messy situation. The people were so desperately sick by the time they got to the tent hospital that it was difficult to help them at all. A large number were dead by the time they were delivered to the medical team.

Many of the local men came out to help, as did a smaller group of local women. In addition to the volunteers, many had loved ones who came with them, and right from the start Sarah instigated a hard-and-fast rule—anyone wishing to remain near a loved one must pitch in and help, and that meant help anyone that needed help, not just their relative. As many of the elderly had no family to assist them, the volunteers and those pressed into service were a blessing. Primarily, the basic treatment consisted of trying to get the fever down. If this was accomplished, it was fairly certain the patient would recover. If the fever refused to break, the outcome was inevitably death. Sarah stated that the disease was definitely not smallpox as there was no rash; the most likely supposition is typhoid, precipitated by the contaminated food and water the people throughout the South had been exposed to for the last several months of the war.

After the first few weeks of operation the team from the North was completely exhausted. It was a twenty-four-hour-a-day job. Nobody ever took eight hours off to sleep; it was just not possible. The fever was no respecter of time and was as likely to break at three in the morning as at three in the afternoon. The nurses simply had to be there, especially for the children. In speaking of the children, Sarah again started to cry: "So many children, it breaks my heart. For the old people it's different. They have lived their lives, but those poor little children; we have lost so many of them. It's driving us crazy. The babies and the three- and four-year-olds, they shoot up a fever and die before we even have a chance to try and help them. Some of them are almost dead by the time they get here. Their parents are a handful, too. It's a hell of a job; it's hard, hard. Underneath it all, I am a fun-loving person. There's nothing I love better than to kick up my heels and have a good time. The thing that keeps me going through all this is looking forward to a time when we can all go back to raising hell and having fun, laughing, singing, dancing, and being in a loving environment again. But we have to do this. It has to be done, and you can't turn your back on it."

They were billeted in the nicer homes in town, and Sarah stayed with a family named Campbell. She could see her host, a rather heavy, rotund man with a round head, possibly named Paul. He treated Sarah and the rest of the Northerners like royalty: "If they don't have what we want, they'd turn over heaven and earth to get it. It was almost embarrassing. We don't dare say we would like something or that we miss something, because by the time we got home from work somehow they'd have managed to find it for us, regardless of the cost or inconvenience. The food was delightful. They are lovely people and I will never, ever forget how wonderfully we were treated!"

The people of Millboro were bewildered and distraught at what was happening to their town. They took turns being extremely grateful to the Northern team for their help and being terribly upset. Until then, their little town had not been through much turmoil. The people of Millboro were spared from active fighting—they had not had their homes burned or their fields razed—but now they were subject to another type of invasion. They were invaded by their neighbors down in the valley who were burned out of their homes, for whom there was really no choice but to come up the mountain. If they had gone east or south, they would have run straight into the war; if they had gone north it would have been into Yankee territory. There was only one direction left them, west, to Millboro. The town was drastically overcrowded; people were camped on every available foot of space, living like animals in sheds and dirt caves, with no sanitation facilities, contaminating the water supplies at every turn. It was no wonder that a terrible epidemic followed. On the heels of the sickness, they were invaded by the medical team, who turned the town into one large hospital. Though they appreciated what the Yankees were doing for them, many despaired that their slow-paced, relaxed, pleasant rural life might become a permanent casualty of the miserable war.

Sarah said: "We are treating everybody, all ages, the old, the young and in between; however, we did not treat any Indians. I think the Indians treated their own sick. They had their own methods and they weren't about to bring their ill to the white man for treatment. Their methods were probably just as good as what we were doing, maybe better. If they had their own remedies we did not know about them, and if we had, I am sure we would not have been allowed to fool with them. The government has their own way of doing things and it isn't always the right way, but that's the way you do it. I am not too aware of the Indians; they stay to themselves in the peripheral area. They were not too interested in helping the white man through the illness; they were more interested in not catching what it was the white man had. We have studied it and decided it is typhoid fever."

Sarah and her group of nurses did not wear uniforms as such, but all wore black skirts, white shirts, lisle stockings, sensible underwear, and low-heeled shoes. Sarah wore her long hair up in a bun and plunged into the hard work that they were geared for. She was, she said: "A take charge type of person, which is not the way I want to be; it's just the way things are turning out. I have a feeling of being very capable." The army did not have a Nurse Corps in those days; the women were employed by the Public Health Service, probably under a contract of some sort. (Author's note: It was the U.S. Sanitary Commission, a privately funded organization.) Sarah commented: "I am on display. I am representing the Union government. We were lectured that we are representing the government, and we and the Union will be judged by how we deport ourselves. This is uppermost in my mind at all times, being a lady and being aware of my demeanor."

Among the first things the medical group noticed when they stepped off the train, in addition to the mountains of supplies, was the large white boarding house. Sarah remarked on the railroad tunnel and said she could see the main street in town and Charley's corral, which she described as much larger than had first been thought. She could see Charley, she said, working with the horses and attempting to train them, in a fashion. One wonders though, now that the war was over, just who he was training them for. She observed that he was a bitter, frustrated man, and it showed very plainly. When asked if she knew Charley, she answered: "Charley and I don't share a common ground." Laughing, she continued: "I don't go into the bars or the gambling hall; I would have no reason to have any liaison with Charley. I am much too busy, and the type of people I affiliate with would be the ones I am staying with or those with whom I work. He is no one I would socialize with at all, not that I am a snob; it's just that he and I travel on different levels. Of course, I realize my stay in town will be limited to the duration of the illness, and I have no goal in making long-term relationships. I like the town, but the work is just awful. All of us are living for the day when we can go home. I love the countryside; it's beautiful and I like the people I've met. Maybe it's because they have put themselves out to be so nice to me. I haven't seen the bad side of anything, but I don't go looking for it."

John, the sheriff, was very much in evidence throughout the epidemic, identified by his ranger-type hat, leather vest, tight pants, and boots with spurs. He gave directions, helped unload wagons, and handled people who got out of hand. Sometimes people would decide that their child needed more treatment, or they wanted their husband or wife closer to the water, or they did not like the way someone was being treated and would try to start trouble. John would simply take them outside, by force if necessary, and explain the facts of life to them. He kept the drinking and carousing down to a minimum in town. He was also very active on the burial detail. Elizabeth said that many of the people who perished in the epidemic were buried out near where her mother was interred, that it was not like a real cemetery until then. This would explain the many unmarked headstones that pepper the hillside today. One of John's children became sick, probably Rachael. Sarah could see him being very concerned and bringing the child into the tent area. She was not too seriously ill, and they were able to get her fever down within a few days and release her.

When asked if there was any political intrigue taking place, Sarah laughed: "Well, the political intrigue is that the North whupped them and the South is not buying it! Sure, they are running around trying to reorganize the Confederacy, but we are not exposed to that because we are Yankees. As far as they are concerned, the war is not really over—they just called a halt while we came down to help them with their sick. There's all kinds of dour looks all over town. Their attitude is that they might have capitulated at Appomattox, but this is not the end. 'The South will rise again'—this is exactly the way they feel."

At the beginning, the food was supplied by the townspeople; the medical team had no facilities to provide for themselves. Food was brought to the tent city in buckets and pans—stews, beans, milk, and bread. After a while a mess tent was set up and soldiers did most of the cooking. The townspeople would bring out meat and raw food, and it would be cooked there in the compound. For the most part it was to feed the medical staff, since a large number of the patients were too ill to handle anything more than soup and milk. Fresh fruit was too acidic to give to the sick, but they were provided with a lot of cheese, eggs, and dairy products. The patients were given some sort of medicine, a white milky fluid, which many of them had trouble keeping down. However bad it got, it was never comparable to the work Sarah had experienced behind the battle-fields. At least the typhoid patients didn't come in missing arms and legs, covered with blood and in agonizing pain.

Toward the end, the extreme work grind tapered off, and the medical team were able to take regular assigned shifts. This gave them time to ride through the woods in buggies, take long walks, and enjoy the beauty of the countryside. The hills were pretty, the town quaint, and with the stench of death diminishing. It was a beautiful place to be. Even with the crisis over, there was little real intermingling, the Northerners still being very cautious and on guard. Despite the fact that the townspeople made them feel welcome and at ease, the team remained reserved and a bit aloof, realizing that's the way it must be. They simply could not get too close to the people in town or become very good friends. The team was grateful for the warm hospitality of the locals, but beyond the mutual cause of the epidemic, there was little common meeting ground. The majority of people in Millboro were farmers and for the most part uneducated and backward. The medical team were all educated, relatively sophisticated people from large cities. They found the antics of the locals extremely amusing at times, but were careful not to be caught laughing at them. They were thoroughly intrigued by the hillbillies of Millboro.

Sarah was attracted to them and at the same time rather horrified by them: "It was a sort of aversion-attraction situation." They had such different attitudes toward things than what she had been accustomed to: "They had cows and that corral right in the center of town, with Charley smacking those horses around next to the railroad. It was such a small potatoes little town, that dumb little mercantile store, all the bars going full bore. We never felt threatened; we weren't around town that much. We got a kick out of it all, like something out of a book. None of us had ever seen anything quite like Millboro before."

About the only outstanding event that Sarah remembered happening while she was in town was Ava's fire: "It was cold, in the winter. I can see smoke and the house going up in flames. It was the event of the year. Even though it was one or two in the morning and pitch black, everyone in town turned out for it. The flames were so high, the fire could be seen for miles away. It was a startling scene that shocked us all, as much as anything in that small town could have." Asked if she had ever met Constance, Sarah saw a flash of orange-red hair and a bright yellow dress. A feeling of repugnance came over her. She later decided that perhaps Constance had made flagrant overtures to one or more of the doctors in the group, and everyone considered her actions offensive.

When the time came to leave Millboro, the parting was very emotional. The medical group left with a great sense of accomplishment and the feeling of much warmth and rapport between themselves and the townspeople, who gave them a rousing sendoff at the train station. Everyone cried. "There was a lot of love exchanged; I think it was because of the war. We came down and gave so much. They were so grateful; they knew we had done everything humanly possible. When the time came, we actually didn't want to go. We loved those people in that town, but we knew it was time to go home. We were just exhausted when we left, but we left with a wonderful feeling in our hearts."

Sarah went home to get married: "He was a tall, handsome man, very well off, perhaps a banker or maybe a doctor." He had waited impatiently for her return from the South. Their first child was a girl and eventually they had two more children. They had a lovely home, and even though she had servants, Sarah did much of the work herself, enjoying every minute of it. She died of pneumonia, quietly and quickly with no pain, in her early or mid sixties. Her children were all grown; her husband had died a few years earlier. She was buried in the family plot; the date on the headstone was 1891.

Looking back on her life, she said there was no question that her wartime services were its highlight. She talked for a long time about the horrors and futility of that war: "What were those people thinking, to bring such a thing upon us all? I am sure that toward the end they asked themselves that same question many times. What a tragedy! Surely the country will heal and become stronger because of it, but that's the only thing that might come out of it that will be worth anything at all."

Looking back on the lifetime of Sarah, I have this to add: For us, the medical team that was sent into Millboro, it was like going into a totally foreign country. The only common denominator was that both sides spoke some derivative of the English language. The young girl I saw very clearly while being hypnotized back to Sarah was the absolute image of my oldest sister, yet my sister and I do not look one bit alike in this lifetime. This is just another aspect of my hypothesis that there exists a genetic or familial component in these past life memories.

# CHAPTER SEVEN

---

# THE INDIANS

---

IT WAS FALL WHEN THE INDIANS were forced out of Robin's Nest, according to Warm Sun: "They walked slowly; they did not want to go. There were soldiers making them leave."

The army did not bother White Bear when they came to move the Indians out. After all, he said: "I was only an Indian in my heart." When asked if he was there when they came to run the Indians off the land, White Bear corrected: "Not run, walk." He watched while the Indians walked out, saying: "They were not happy to move." He described how the Indians, mostly women and children, moved slowly as they dragged their belongings behind them on sleds made of sticks and skins. They were herded out, the braves going first. A great many of the Indian men "ran" into the woods, promising their families that later they would come and get them, but of course they never did. Several of the men who had run were caught and made to go with the rest. Most of the older men and very young ones went of their own volition. It was pathetic, he claimed, "to see the women carrying the little children and trying to drag their belongings behind them."

White Bear: "I feel that there were three different tribes represented in Robin's Nest, but they all lived under the same governing body, one chief." Perhaps it was around 1874 when the Indians were forced out, although he had no real way of remembering time, having grown up living in a cave since he was about seven years old. He did not relate much to what was happening elsewhere. When he was about fifty, White Bear died alone on the top of his mountain. The sun was warm, the sky blue. He was very tired, decided it was time to die, and he did. It was as simple as that.

Making an effort to rebuild his life in Millboro, John found it impossible. Everywhere he turned, he saw Becky. Every time he looked at his children, he was forced to face his own involvement in her death. By the time the epidemic was over and once the children had all been settled into new homes, he left town one day, never to return. He went to reclaim his Indian roots, at first staying with Indian groups in Virginia, then later making his way to the Dakotas and joining the Sioux tribe there. The Indians gave him the name "Two Man," which was probably a way of designating his dual background, part white and part Indian.

When the Indians from Robin's Nest were evacuated by U.S. government troops, Little Eagle became a "runner." Rather than submit to relocation, he simply melted into the forest and continued to live in the woods. Liz cried as she remembered how the Indians were herded out by men in uniforms on horseback carrying rifles. They were made to walk, like cattle. She received word of John from time to time through Little Eagle, who kept in close contact with the Indian underground.

In 1876, John, together with most of the braves of the Sioux tribe, left for Montana to keep an appointment with destiny and George Armstrong Custer at the Little Big Horn.

Barbara stated that George Armstrong Custer had something to do with the Indians being moved onto the reservations. It was somehow involved with his aspirations to be president.

*Old photo of Millboro in the 1800s*

*Katy's Tunnel*

*Honey's boarding house*

*Foundation of the stairs Becky used to sneak into Charley's room*

*Church standing on site of Becky's old house*

*Joe supports a large
foundation stone that
came from Becky's
house*

*Constance's house, still in good condition*

*Foundation of old railroad station*

*Old saloon and gambling hall, now Millboro General Store*

*Honey's boarding house in 1800s, seen through railroad depot*

*Shed where John and Samuel used to meet*

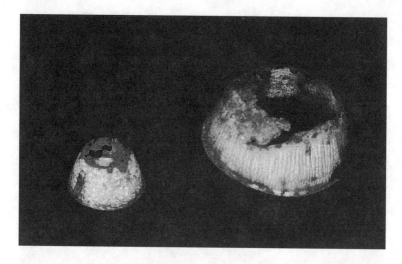

*Remains of Becky's Graniteware cup and bowl*

*Little family plot where all claim Becky is buried*

*Remains of old mill on the Cowpasture River*

*Old Confederate fort in Millboro*

# CHAPTER EIGHT

## GOING TO MILLBORO

THIS ENTIRE STORY SEEMED VERY ABSTRACT until we actually went back to Millboro. As Maureen, Joe, and I drove toward Millboro in a rented car in the spring of 1987, the excitement and suspense in the air had built up to a high pitch. Each of us was engulfed in our own thoughts, wondering what we were really looking for. I had told Maureen and Joe, not being totally serious when I said it, not to be surprised if half the people back there don't still call it "Marlboro"! We were driving the highway from Warm Springs, and you curve right to drive into Millboro. As we weren't very sure about it, we stopped for a soda pop and asked if we were on the right road. The man said: "Yes, just keep going to the right and it'll take you right into Marlboro." We all started laughing; it really broke the tension. I was remembering the first days when Maureen and I were looking for Marlboro on the map and couldn't find it, then Maureen said: "There's a little town of Millboro—could that be it?"

Rounding the curve heading into town from the direction of Warm Springs, we could hardly contain our apprehension. Although we had all discussed the fact that the Millboro of 1987 would not look like the Millboro of the 1860s, subconsciously Maureen and Joe were expecting to see it through the eyes of Becky and Charley. I, myself, really didn't know what to expect.

After passing a yellow building with the sign "Millboro General Store" in front, I said: "Oh, we're here!" There was a new brick building across the street, which is the post office. Joe kept on driving for another mile or so, and we started curving up the hill on the way to where the Robin's Nest area would be. I told Joe: "I think we just went through the heart of town!" He was aghast and said: "We couldn't have—there's nothing there!" But of course the general store was there, so we went back to the general store and went in. The man there said: "Yes, this is Millboro; this is all there is." Joe asked: "But where are all the buildings?" I reminded him that was 130 years ago; they are no longer here!

It was a shock, especially for Maureen and Joe who had spent the past several months viewing, in their minds, Millboro as it once was. The wooden buildings that lined the streets were gone, and only a concrete foundation remained of the railroad station. With the exception of the general store and the new post office building, everything else was either deserted or had disappeared completely. Earlier in the study Millie Sproule, entranced into the lifetime of Honey, had stated that her boarding house had been ripped down and no longer existed. This turned out to be virtually the only statement, made under hypnosis, regarding Millboro that was proven false.

We were all standing by the remains of the railroad station, and I pointed at this big green building and said: "Joe, is there any chance that this could have been the old boarding house?" He got the funniest look on his face and said: "No, but my God! That bright red one next to it sure as hell is! It used to be white." When we got a little closer, we could see the red paint peeling off to display white paint underneath.

Next to the boarding house is a small building Maureen identified as the former barber shop that she and Constance so assiduously avoided. Next to it is a red brick building that was once a bank. Some of the local people say it was there during the Civil War, but I have since discovered otherwise. Joe and Maureen claim that all the buildings back then were wooden and that the boarding house was most likely the only one painted. According to Joe and

Maureen, the bank in the 1860s was wooden and very small. They laughed over the time the bank's first heavy-duty vault had arrived in town: "It was brought in on a flatbed or train car. They tried to haul it with a wagon, but it broke the wagon, so they hitched up several teams of horses and literally dragged it through town to the bank."

Looking down the railroad tracks leading out of town, one sees Katy's Tunnel. The raised lettering above the mouth of the tunnel is weather beaten and partly obliterated, but you can still make out the words "Millboro Tunnel." Very early in this study, we had sent for a map of Bath County, and one of the first things I noticed was a label "Millboro Tunnel." When I mentioned this to Maureen, she immediately said: "Katy's Tunnel," so I asked why she called it that and she replied: "I don't know; we just always called it Katy's Tunnel." I spoke to one man in Millboro who was a Civil War buff about why the tunnel was called Katy's Tunnel, and he said: "There was this engineer that worked on the railroad; his name was Cady. The railroad thought perhaps the tunnel had been named for him." Then we were told that the man who ran the post office was quite a local historian, so I went to talk with him. I said: "I'm going to ask you a question. I think I already know the answer. Why do they call it 'Katy's Tunnel'?" He got this satirical look on his face and started to grin, and I said: "You don't even have to answer—I already know."

Crossing over the tracks on a high wooden bridge and turning left, we drove a block or two down the road and came to Constance's house. In regressions, the house had been described as painted brown with grey trim. It was now yellow. Maureen and Joe claimed that a couple of rooms had been added onto the back. It was uninhabited when we found it, but by peeking through the windows we decided that it had been recently occupied by several families at once. On closer inspection the yellow paint was found to be peeling, and we could see the brown paint and grey trim showing through.

By now our excitement had mounted, running around from place to place. Although much had been knocked down, fallen down, burned down, and otherwise changed, it was still in some ways amazingly untouched by time. As more original pieces of the puzzle became real, emotions that had been held in check, waiting to see what might actually be there, began to surface.

Heading out of town in the direction of Warm Springs, as we passed the general store again, Joe slammed on the brakes and announced: "That used to be the saloon and gambling parlor!" We stopped and got out to talk to the present owners, who confirmed that yes, in the old days it was a saloon. Joe hadn't recognized it at first because it used to be longer. A fire had demolished one end of the building at some time, and the owner, rather than rebuild, had simply sealed off that end. A lean-to shed stands at that end today.

Continuing down the road with Maureen directing us, we rounded a bend, made a sharp right turn, and entered a driveway that led to a tall, white, Baptist church nestled in the woods a long way from the road. This was the church that had been described by Becky, Elizabeth, and others as standing today where Becky's house used to be. Joe and Maureen both became very emotional looking at that site. I was fascinated to see that the church was exactly as had been described—the high steeple, tall steps, white clapboard with large grey bricks on the bottom. Both Constance's house and Becky's property were just as Constance and Becky had described them while hypnotized. Leaving the site of Becky's house, we passed the place where Jake Bauer was hung. There is a tree in that spot today, but it seems unlikely that it's the same tree; it didn't seem large enough.

The next day we returned to the boarding house and discovered to our delight that the tenants were home and willing to let us walk around inside and videotape. Maureen had gone down the road to look at something, so Joe and I climbed the large outside steps and walked around to the front of the building. Pointing to a bedroom window, Joe announced that had been his room when he lived there as Charley. He said there had been a swing mounted on the porch at one time. Searching, we found two screws still embedded in the wood that would have supported the swing. About this time, Maureen rejoined us and I asked her to lead us to Charley's room.

Without so much as a look over her shoulder, she went around the corner and said: "Here's the room, on the corner, where he used to be. This window here is where I used to sneak in." Then she called our attention to the remaining foundation that once supported another set of steps leading to the upper porch. They ended right next to the window that she used when entering Charley's room. She used those steps a lot and mentioned them in regressions often, because they were on the far side, and she felt she was less likely to be seen by anyone.

When we entered the old boarding house, we discovered that the upper rooms had been renovated into living quarters occupied by a young couple with a small child. They were in the process of moving out and informed us that the house had just been bought by a Mr. Pelter. The rear bedroom had been converted into a kitchen, the front room was a living room, and the rest remained as bedrooms. We looked through them, and Joe stated that they were virtually unchanged from Civil War days. When we entered Charley's old room upstairs, the air was charged with emotion, Maureen had tears in her eyes and Joe had a very intense look on his face. Joe remarked that the door handles and other hardware were the same as when Charley lived there.

The downstairs area was in a state of disrepair. What had been the dining room of Honey's restaurant was intact, but the ceiling looked as though it might cave in at any moment. Joe and Maureen pointed out the place where Honey had a small bar set up in the rear and where, against a far wall, a piano player had played an old upright nightly, his back to the diners. There was a smaller room off the dining room and a much larger room to the rear that had been Honey's kitchen. The lower section of the house was boarded up, and it was too dark in the rear to see anything.

Walking around outside to the back of the building, we found a concrete foundation covered with boards and rubble. Joe and Maureen claimed that this had been the blacksmith's shop where Charley had taken his horses to be shod. Walking down the alley toward the big green building, Joe outlined for us the perimeters of Charley's horse corral. Pointing to an area in the rear of deep, dark green lush grass, he claimed that on that spot was where Charley had piled a large mound of horse manure!

Returning to Constance's old house, we circled around it once more, and Maureen pointed out where she had been sitting on the porch railing one day when Mr. Waverly, Constance's father, happened by. Waving his stick at her, he declared that it was unladylike and unbecoming for Becky to be perched on a porch railing like a child! She added that he carried that stick with him at all times, shaking it menacingly at anything or anybody that crossed him or got in his way.

At this point I placed Maureen in a state I call "walking hypnosis." Her eyes would be open, she would be able to walk and talk normally, but she would be in a deep hypnotic state that allowed her to see two time frames at once. She would see things as they were in the present, right in front of her, and superimposed on that, things as they were in Becky's time, similar to a double exposed photograph, two pictures, one on top of the other. This technique worked very well with both Maureen and Joe and later with Barbara. The only minor problem was that Maureen sometimes became very exuberant and difficult to control. She was inclined to run off on her own to explore things by herself, while Joe and I, usually toting cameras and trying to videotape, would be left in the dust. I eventually solved the problem by hanging on to her arm or the tail of her shirt tightly, so she could not launch out on her own!

After placing Maureen in this dual time frame, I asked her to lead us from Constance's house to where Ava's house had been before it burned down. She immediately took off down the road at top speed, me hot on her tail and Joe struggling to keep up, hauling a very heavy video camera. She ran down the road to where it curved to go over a bridge (over the railroad tracks), then she swerved a little to the left and headed down a very narrow, overgrown, almost indistinguishable buggy road. After running down this weedy path for a few hundred feet, she suddenly turned sharply left and plunged into a huge thicket of brush. I followed up to where I thought she had disappeared and likewise plunged into the brush. Suddenly I was standing in a large clearing, cut by an old unused driveway leading up to the stone foundation where a house once stood. The clearing had not grown over, and you could almost feel the intense fire that had once burned here. Even the topmost branches of the trees surrounding the house area still looked charred and burned. Catching up with Maureen, I found her seated beside a large creek at the rear of the clearing, busily removing her shoes and socks. Inquiring: "Where are you going Becky?" she answered: "Oh, I'm going to lead you down to the waterfall." It was May and it was cold—neither Joe nor I were really up for strolling down the stream—but we could hear the waterfall, and when I go back, I'm going to get some pictures of it. Certainly there is a waterfall down by that stream, and she knew all about it. They all knew about that waterfall!

Driving back to where Becky's house had stood, walking around to the rear of the church, I spotted an interesting wooden structure across a ravine near the creek. Becky said: "That's the feed box; John built it to feed the stock." As she continued to walk around the side of the church nearest the woods, she said: "This is where I made the soap, because it stinks!" explaining that it was far enough away from the house that the fumes did not permeate it. Wandering around in the woods surrounding Becky's house, we made several amazing discoveries. Right at the edge of the forest there were several large, squared off stones that Joe said had been the foundation stones under the house.

Walking on into the woods, I slipped on the remains of a large, graniteware cup; a little further on Maureen and Joe found a matching bowl. Later we discovered an old liniment bottle, rose colored from age. Maureen said it was identical to the one Becky had used to clobber Jake during his fight with John, except it was a little shorter. These items we saved and I still have them. After we returned to our rooms, Becky explained that the graniteware bowl was one she used for her home pot stew made of beef and vegetables. The stew was made in a larger kettle, and John was served in that large bowl; there were smaller bowls of the same graniteware for her and the kids. She remembered when John had brought home the brand new graniteware set for her: "In a very large carton; he had bartered something for it." The cup we found she kept tied to the tree by the spring, so the children could get a drink when they were outside playing. Occasionally when Charley came to the house, he would untie it and use it to drink coffee from. This used to irritate her to no end: "That cup was to be used for water; there were cups in the house for coffee." A few days later in the town of Staunton we authenticated the graniteware. It had been made in 1830 in England and in 1860 in America, so the time was exactly right for Becky to have a new set.

While in Millboro we were fortunate to meet Ralph, a young man who has made an extensive study of the Civil War, particularly as it applied to the Millboro area. Ralph showed us an old Civil War gun emplacement, still intact, on the edge of town. While Joe, Ralph, and I were examining the old wooden fortification, Maureen, in a walking trance, slipped off and disappeared, reappearing about the time she was missed. Later that evening under hypnosis I asked her if there was anything in Millboro that we had missed. She answered: "The old shed where Samuel met with John. But it's all right; we got a picture of it." Joe and I puzzled over this until after our return to Lake Elsinore and Maureen's film was developed. There was a photo, clear as life, of an old shed that neither Joe nor myself had seen. When Maureen showed her photos to Smokey Williamson (Samuel), he immediately pulled that picture out of the pile and exclaimed: "That's the old shed, where I used to meet John!"

After Maureen's disappearance that day, Joe and I kept a more careful eye on her while she was in the walking hypnosis state. There was one incident when she nearly ran casually into the middle of the road, oblivious of traffic, but Joe caught her arm before she got into the street. When conscious, she explained that she hadn't even noticed the sound of approaching automobiles because she was listening for the clip-clop of horses' hooves.

Every evening Joe and Maureen would be regressed back into their former lives in Millboro. One evening Charley spoke briefly about the help the Indians had been to him in his forays into the hills. He claimed that he frequently encountered the stills dotted all over, and if you stumbled on one, no one ever bothered to check credentials. It was assumed they were government agents up to no good and they were shot. This coincided with what Warm Sun had stated, that there was a special graveyard high in those hills where they buried "revenuers." The Indians were of immense help to Charley—they knew where everything was and what was going on in those hills at all times. He rewarded them liberally, sometimes with tobacco, then he added, making an awful face: "Can you believe they swallowed that stuff?!"

Charley also described an overabundance of troops guarding the railroad tunnels at either end. The Confederacy, he said, "had troops all over hell" in the area of Millboro, in the woods, and on the flatlands. At night there were fires everywhere. It was a common sight to see four or five soldiers bathing in a stream with one or two armed soldiers standing guard. He continued: "They threw up a pile of housing for the Headquarters Command. They were down off a back road; they did not want them too near the townspeople. It was necessary to go through two or three sentries to reach them. Every time they found somebody who knew something about wood and could drive a nail, they threw up more housing for the officers. Housing and a big war room for planning."

In addition to the soldiers having taken over the town, Charley reiterated that the whole town was a mess: "The supplies were all over, mountains of supplies, more goods than they could ever use and more coming in all the time on the train. Wagons were going out of there constantly, night and day. They were desperately trying to get the supplies to Roanoke or Lynchburg so they could be taken on to Richmond to supply the line, the line that was trying to hold Richmond."

This is something that seemed odd to me as I conducted this research. Having looked in every book I could find on the Civil War, never once was there any reference to the town of Millboro and it's importance to the war. Only in one book was the town ever mentioned and that was in *Virginia Railroads in the Civil War* (University of North Carolina Press, Chapel Hill, 1961). Now, I remember reading that Lee's last desperate thrust, when he was leaving Richmond and Grant was chasing him, was to get to Lynchburg where he could get his supplies. Well, these supplies were probably coming down from Millboro!! That's where the trains unloaded; that's why there were all those soldiers at the tunnels. It was absolutely crucial to the Confederate war effort, and yet there is no mention of it in the Civil War books.

From *Virginia Railroads in the Civil War*, by Angus James Johnston, II, p. 34 and 35:

> The railroads and senseless regulations however, were not alone to blame for the failure to supply the armies with food. A major factor was the laxity in the military in promptly unloading cars. Some Quartermasters habitually looked upon freight cars as storage facilities, never realizing that future supplies would not be forthcoming until the cars were released. An investigation by Secretary of War, Judah P. Benjamin, in September 1861, revealed that a few days previously as many as thirteen trains, eleven of them fully loaded, had been allowed to collect at Manassas Junction. At about the same time, the lack of warehouse facilities at Millborough, the temporary western terminus of the Virginia Central Railroad, tied up fifty cars, approximately one-fourth of the company's rolling stock. Superintendent Whitcomb, explaining why the road could not immediately ship 1,000 barrels of flour on September 18, alluded to the situation at Millborough. . . .

Another problem mentioned was:

> . . . the red clay roads in the wet fall and winter seasons. Inasmuch as the six-mule teams ate almost as much as they could haul through the mud, which was generally two feet deep. . . .

Fifty cars! This amount of matériel suddenly unloaded from these cars must have boggled the mind; it's no wonder everyone in the study mentioned it. Maureen was positively jubilant when I found that item because she had told me very early on that the town was originally spelled "Millborough." She said: "See, I told you they used to spell it that way!"

But the real mystery, as I've said, was why the Union troops didn't make a major effort to get to Millboro and seize the supplies. When they were burning out the Shenandoah Valley, Lynchburg is on one side of the Shenandoah Valley and Millboro is on the other. There's a direct route; I think it is now highway 39. That's where they were jumping the supply wagons. They didn't usually kill the drivers, but they would turn over the wagons and confiscate their goods. One would think they would be motivated to venture into the hills and locate the source of these supplies.

They did have troops on the outskirts of Millboro because there was a skirmish near Becky's house, something like two hundred yards away. Becky said that she could hear the sounds, but I don't think she was aware at the time of how close it was, and in any case, she said she and the kids didn't realize it was actual shooting. Becky's house was on the eastern edge of town, and Ralph, the Civil War historian, said that there was some shooting on the

*Joe points to hole drilled by Charley in 1864.*

*Hole near entrance of tunnel, covered by mortar*

outskirts of town, but that's the closest the Union Army ever got! You can speculate endlessly, but I don't suppose there will ever be a real concrete answer as to why they didn't go into Millboro.

## CHARLEY'S MISSION TO MILLBORO

One evening while still in Millboro, Joe was regressed back to the life of Charley and remembered a night when he and John got to drinking together. In a reckless moment, Charley told John what he thought of the affair with Rose and how much it was hurting Becky. John, of course, told Charley in no uncertain terms to mind his own business. When reminded of his own affair, Charley swore that John never knew of the romance with Becky. If anyone were foolish enough to say anything derogatory about Becky within John's hearing, as Jake had done the day Becky broke the bottle over his head, John would turn on them belligerently. So the townspeople kept their silence; however, despite what Constance claimed, Charley insisted that few people in town knew. Honey knew of course, but she was closemouthed. It did come as a big surprise, however, when Charley learned that Liz, John's mother, knew all about it.

Charley said that Rose showed up in town after the war had already started and that occasionally she left the bordello to come to Honey's boarding house to meet John. John always pretended that he did not know that Rose was coming and would put on an act of being upset to see her there. After this had happened a few times, Charley began to have suspicions that there was more to this than just an affair, that perhaps Rose was a contact for John. He had already begun to strongly suspect that John was involved in spy activities for the North. Charley said and did nothing about this hunch, not out of concern for Becky as might be assumed, but because he was working on learning who the other contacts were. It must be remembered that Charley was a fanatic when it came to the Southern cause. In his mind, nothing took precedence over a victory for the Confederacy, no matter what sacrifices had to be made. Charley himself, as it turned out, sacrificed a great deal more than anyone ever realized.

Charley did catch one man who seemed suspicious to him, a salesman claiming to be just passing through Millboro. The man talked to Charley about seeds and horse liniment. Sensing something was not quite right about the man, Charley searched him on the spot and uncovered a packet of Union money, which was incriminating in itself, but he also found an unsigned letter containing "Advisements" on some of the current existing problems in Millboro. The man was turned over to the Confederate Army and taken, under guard, to Richmond for interrogation.

The three of us spent a good deal of time going through local cemeteries searching for—we really were not sure what. We spent hours at the historic, old Windy Cove Presbyterian Church in Millboro Springs, studying the gravestones in the churchyard. This is one of the oldest churches and cemeteries in America; it was built in the mid 1700s. Charley kept insisting that Becky was buried on the other side of town in a small cemetery, roughly a mile or so outside of town. He said her grave was enclosed in a compound, surrounded by short iron fencing. Liz had once observed: "Becky's grave is now neglected and all overgrown with weeds." I tended to listen to Liz as Barbara Roberts had shown a lot of psychic ability during this study. I was interested to see if her prediction would come true. She had told me I would find a picture of Charley in a book, and she also said that there was a record of Becky's death somewhere but didn't know if I would find it.

The next day we were driving on the other side of town, looking for some sign of the old church that was reported to have been out there, when suddenly we spotted some graves on the side of a hill sloping down from the road. The entire area was sorely neglected and overgrown with weeds. Maureen wouldn't go down with us to investigate; she stayed near the car. Joe and I walked down the slope. Suddenly he walked right to a little rectangle of iron fencing (it looked like a family plot) and he said: "This is where Becky's buried. It used to be bigger; they've made it smaller." When I looked closely, I found where some of the metal had been cut. There were two standing monuments there; the name on them was "Ailstock." Joe led me to an unmarked site along one side of the fencing and stated: "She's buried right down there."

Maureen had been wandering about the hillside and refused to come into the Ailstock compound. In an adjoining area were headstones marked "Pelter." Later, when we found members of the Ailstock family, they told us that the entire area of those compounds is referred to as "the Pelter plot." The unexpected discovery of Becky's grave was very upsetting to both Joe and Maureen. Maureen would not talk about it at all, and Joe couldn't seem to stop talking about it. That evening back in the hotel, while in the conscious state, Joe proceeded to relive the entire funeral. There were about seventeen people present, and as they stood at the gravesite listening to a minister droning on and on, Charley began to hate the man. It was a bitter cold day and by far the saddest in anyone's memory. He described Honey, standing off to one side, dressed in a long grey skirt with a fitted black coat up to her neck and a large black hat. In her arms she held baby Peter, who looked around at everything and everybody with curiosity, having no idea of what was happening. By her feet were two or three of Becky's other children, and Honey was sobbing uncontrollably, as were most of the other mourners.

Joe talked for hours that night, trying to come to terms with the time when the brightest light in Charley's life was extinguished for good. That bleak January day marked a tragedy not only for Becky and her loved ones, but for the whole town of Millboro, which had apparently never dealt with this sort calamity before. It traumatized the entire town and no one's life was ever quite the same.

We spent an afternoon in the Bath County courthouse going through what old records there were, to no avail. We were unaware at that time that there had been a fire in the courthouse in the early 1900s, and the records from that period were either destroyed or badly damaged. An afternoon was also spent in Staunton, perusing microfilm of the two weekly newspapers of the time, looking for any mention of Becky's murder or the hanging of Jake Bauer. Although we had no luck, the old newspapers did make interesting reading. The largest part of each paper was devoted to a lengthy treatise about the righteous cause of the South. We found absolutely no mention of the assassination of President Lincoln in the papers after the Civil War; the only clue that it had happened was that the articles shifted from castigating Lincoln to berating President Johnson. It was easy to understand William Tecumseh Sherman's aversion to and mistrust of the journalists of the time. A great deal of space in those papers detailed Confederate troop movements, which outfits had left, which were packing up and preparing to depart, when they would depart, and where they were departing to. Military censorship of the press was obviously unknown then. Filling in space in all the papers were innumerable racist jokes all aimed at "niggers," complete with appropriate patois. Soon after the war's end, there were several highly indignant articles vehemently denying that Jefferson Davis, president of the now defunct Confederacy, had ever masqueraded as a woman to avoid capture by Union troops.

Then something happened that changed the complexion of the entire story. We were talking with Ralph, the Civil War buff, when he casually remarked that it was rumored that there had been a school for Confederate spies in Millboro during the war. Suddenly a very bright light went on in my head. Throughout this entire project, I had wondered something about Charley: why would the Confederate Army turn a man with five years of training at West Point out of the service because of what appeared to be superficial wounds? Many men on both sides in that war continued to fight actively after losing arms and legs. It seemed plausible that, at least, considering his extensive training at the most elite military academy in the country, they would have put him behind a desk at Richmond.

That evening I hypnotized Joe and inquired of Charley where he had first gone when his wounds had healed and if he had met with any important people. He answered that he was sitting around a large, round table with several men. He was wearing a dress uniform. All of the men except one were wearing grey uniforms; one man was wearing civilian clothing. Then he clammed up, stating that this was top secret military material that he could discuss with no one. As Joe came out of the trance, a look of confusion and total amazement came over his face. He said: "That's what's changed! I was still in uniform when I met with those men! I was never out of the army!!"

At this point a whole new memory came flooding back to him. He had given me clues back at the beginning, when we first started working on this study and I asked him his name. He said his name was Charley Morgan but had said: "I had another name earlier." What I didn't realize was that Charley Morgan was his name—when he was in Millboro! Once we took him back to these vivid memories prior to Millboro, everything began to change.

Charley recalled: "I was getting either briefed or debriefed, talking to some really high-ranking people. I swear I was talking to Jeb Stuart and, could it be, General Lee? Stuart and Lee were both 'point men.' There was a man in civies who was clean shaven; the rest, except for Jeb, had beards. Stuart had a handlebar moustache. The meeting was in somebody's house, around a large, round oak table. I was being put into something called 'Special Branch'; we did not call it 'Intelligence.' There was a man with a real cavernous face there." (Later he stated that he didn't think Lee was there, but there were certainly some high-ranking Confederate officers, and the man with the cavernous face might have been Secretary of War Seddon.)

Charley was being promoted and given a very important responsibility: he was ordered to Millboro, Virginia, with a cover identity as a civilian horse trainer. He had very specific orders: "To secure the railroad, blow it up, also the two tunnels if the Yankees ever threatened to take Millboro." This was Charley's undercover mission to Millboro!!

With the tunnels destroyed, there would be no way for the Union to move the supplies out if they took the town. Charley stated that if those supplies had fallen into Yankee hands and they could have moved them out of Millboro, the war would have been over for the South in a matter of weeks. At this meeting, he was given a letter signed by Jefferson Davis, authorizing him to seize command of the Millboro area at any time he deemed it to be necessary and automatically promoting him to the rank of general at the same time. The letter had a seal on it that would have been impossible to counterfeit. Charley kept it in his inner coat pocket; when he got to Millboro, he carefully wrapped the letter in a piece of leather and buried it under a large rock for later retrieval. He added that after the war, he burned the letter as it was highly incriminating and would have gotten him shot "in a heartbeat." Upon leaving the meeting, the civilian, who Joe believes was Jefferson Davis, said to him: "These are desperate and trying times. You cannot fail at this mission. It will greatly enhance our cause. Good luck and God bless you." Then they shook hands.

Most of the other military personnel stationed at Millboro were unaware of Charley's real identity or of the significance of the tunnels. "Without that train and that station, the South did not have a prayer," he stated, adding that all his "hunting" trips into the hills were actually reconnaissance missions to size up the military situation.

When Charley first went to Millboro, early in the war, he was complacent, sure that the fight would be won by the South in a matter of three or four months. Then as the war dragged on and there was a minor skirmish just outside of town (the one near Becky's house, which has been historically established) in 1864, resulting in the death of two soldiers, he began to get nervous. Rounding up a detail of men, he led them into the two tunnels where they spent several days drilling strategically placed holes on either side of the tunnel walls, approximately seven feet from the ground and spaced every thirty feet or so apart. They were staggered, so that one hole was centered between the two across from it.

After carefully removing a brick, the holes were drilled about two and a half inches in diameter and about fourteen inches deep to hold a pipe bomb made of gun powder. Charley had plenty of fuse wire, which he would have looped from one charge across the tunnel to another. It would have been necessary for him to be on the hillside on top of the tunnel to detonate the fuse. He said he would have to "light the fuse and run like hell!" Then he stated that the holes are still there, in Katy's Tunnel! The ones near the front of the tunnel had been plastered over, but the holes in the center are still visible.

The next morning we could hardly wait to finish breakfast, go buy a flashlight, and head for the tunnels. I must say, Katy's Tunnel is not a place where anyone would want to spend much time; it's pitch black in there and the flashlight was not much help. It's cold and very damp, the walls seep water, and there is always about five or six inches of water on the tunnel floor. To add to the thrill, a diesel train roars through, unannounced, periodically. It's definitely not a place in which to linger.

Soon after entering the tunnel, we found places where the bricks had been mortared over. Plunging deeper into the tunnel, we came upon holes exactly as Joe had described them the night before. A brick had been carefully removed, and we could faintly see a circle in the center of the space where the brick had been. These were the holes that Charley and his detail of men had drilled in those walls in the year 1864!

Except for the missing bricks, the tunnel walls appeared to be in excellent condition, no visible deterioration, no chipped or cracked bricks. Liz had stated: "The Indians in Robin's Nest made the bricks that were used to build the tunnels. They ground up some extremely tough grass that grew nearby and added it to the mixture. The bricks were virtually indestructible."

Charley said that he had hidden the bulk of the blasting powder and detonating wire under Becky's house! When asked if he was really willing to risk the life of the woman he loved and her children by storing explosives under her house, he answered: "I would have gladly blown up Millboro and the entire state of Virginia if it would have meant winning the war for the South." It was not difficult to understand why this man was chosen for this particular mission to Millboro.

On our last evening in Millboro, Ralph came to our rooms and I regressed Maureen and Joe back into the lives of Becky and Charley. Ralph, talking to Charley, asked about some of the outfits that had been in Millboro during the war. Charley said: "The 47th Virginia Cavalry rings a bell. I remember some funny uniforms; they looked like Hessians, always putting their pants inside their socks." Becky mentioned an officer named "Chandler," and Charley added: "Chandler was a 1st lieutenant." Charley came to Millboro in 1862, he said: "It was a sergeant who gave me the vouchers; I remember a Captain Tutweiller's signature on the vouchers. The Commissary Officer was. . . ." Becky said: "It was an 'O' or a 'T.' Orr, that was the name." Charley stated: "I kept a very low profile and didn't deal with anyone under the rank of Lt. Colonel."

Ralph asked Charley where he went on his hunting trips. Charley said: "I did a wheel; I was watching movements." Then Ralph asked who owned the general store. Becky answered: "Either Jefferies or Warren." Asked if there was a permanent fort of any type in town, Charley said: "There were star outposts." In response to another of Ralph's questions, regarding a line of trenches near the east entrance to the tunnel, Charley responded: "Oh, yeah, it was on the thicket side, on my left when facing the tunnel, near Constance's house, only further out. They had trenches all over the area; for security purposes they had to." Charley recalled: "Once in a while I would make contact with field grade. It was hard to get messages out and very dangerous to my cover; that was why I sent messages in code and dealt only with high ranks. The troops moved about a lot, but hopefully the information got back to Richmond." In the conscious state, they talked about the Star Fort and decided it was called so because the fortifications were in the shape of a star. Ralph said that all the answers the two had given him were either correct or very close to being correct. Joe admitted: "When Ralph started asking questions, I was suspicious of him and was less inclined to answer."

The day we left Millboro to return home, Ralph presented us with some priceless old photographs of Millboro probably taken sometime after the Civil War. There are no soldiers evident in the photos, but in the foreground one can plainly see Charley's corral, as well as the train depot and the general store. Using a magnifying glass to read the sign outside the store, it reads: "W.C. Warren, Dealer in General Merchandise." Becky had said that the store owner owned a lot of land, and Charley had muttered under his breath: "He has lousy prices, too!" This amused Ralph. Charley admitted: "I only jacked up the prices of my horses to certain people. If they were not true to the cause, then the price went up." In one photo, taken through the train loading platform, you can clearly see the big white boarding house that belonged to Honey.

## CHAPTER NINE

---

# SALT LAKE CITY, UTAH

---

SEARCHING FOR BIRTH AND DEATH RECORDS in the county seat at Warm Springs, Virginia, was an unrewarding task. We did unearth a death certificate for Lucinda Ailstock and for a while thought we had found Liz. Barbara Roberts (Liz) kept insisting that Lucinda did not seem right, and after tracking down some of Lucinda's descendants, it was discovered that she had given birth to ten children, so that premise was abandoned. It was in the Genealogical Library of the Church of the Latter-day Saints in Salt Lake City, Utah, that some documentation began to come to light. It is difficult to document that time period in and around Millboro—records are very sketchy, incomplete, and probably inaccurate in many cases, due largely to the fire mentioned earlier.

In the census book for Virginia, 1850, there is listed an Eliza Ailstock. Eliza is a name that could easily be shortened to Liz, and when Liz was asked about the name, she made a face of sheer repugnance, explaining: "That's a terrible name!" It was, however, her name, she admitted, but she hated it and stated that she would rather have even been called "girl," which is what her uncle had always called her. (A few years earlier, the book *Uncle Tom's Cabin* had been published, in which the beleaguered heroine was a little Negro girl named Eliza. This connection upset Liz.) The Ailstock man she married took delight in calling her "Lizzie," which definitely increased her hatred of him.

In the Mormon libraries in both Salt Lake City, Utah, and Hemet, California, there exist records of Elizabeth Ailstock's marriage to a John Thacker in 1868. There was no way of knowing if this was Becky's Elizabeth, however, until Diana Lovegren (Elizabeth) was asked if the name John Thacker meant anything to her, and she asked in return: "Was he my husband?"

Studying the microfilm records of the Bath County vital records, birth and death registers 1853–1870, the following was discovered: the birth of baby Peter R. Ailstock in 1859 to Andrew and Mary Jane Ailstock and the death on January 22, 1867, of Mary Jane Ailstock (misspelled "Meary"), wife of Andrew, of "unknown" causes, at the age of thirty. Although there are a number of death records listing "unknown" as the cause of death, none of them were a young woman in her thirties.

These particular records are not photostats of actual death and birth certificates; they are simple lists, written by hand, possibly a long time after the actual events occurred. It is my opinion that the birth record for baby Peter is correct except for the year, as he was approximately two years old when his mother was killed, making his birth date around 1862. The death of Mary Jane (Becky) is also two years too late. This date may have inadvertently been changed in the copying of records, or it may have been deliberately doctored. Many people in the study had stated that if a death record were found for Becky, the cause of death would be altered or not listed because the Ailstock family was bent on covering up the real cause of her death. What probably happened is that the records were damaged in the fire in such a way that there was a lot of guessing done on dates and other information when an attempt was made to recreate them.

The origin of the Ailstock name is a real mystery. One of the Ailstock descendants stated that it was English; however, several of the experts in name origin in the Mormon library insist that it is not. Their opinion is that it could possibly be French, but it is most probably Swedish. Some of the older tombstones in Millboro spell the name "Aylstock." When the name was shown to Becky and Liz while in trance, they both identified it as theirs. Becky pronounced it "Aishtick," saying that the *l* is silent, while Liz pronounced it "Aushlick." On our second trip to Millboro we met with several members of the Ailstock family, and one of the women volunteered that her grandmother had pronounced it "Aushlick" all her life.

Liz said that John's real name was indeed Andrew, but she had called him John from the beginning. He was named Andrew after an illustrious Ailstock ancestor, and while Liz said she liked the name because it sounded strong, she was perhaps secretly rebelling against the memory of the hated Ailstock husband and his family by choosing a name of her own. According to records in Salt Lake City, there was also another young Andrew Ailstock in town at the time who later married a woman named Susan. In the records at Salt Lake City were found several references to Levy Ailstock, who appeared to be about the same age as John. Liz identified Levy as a cousin of John's, probably the one referred to by people in the study as "Jeff." Levy and John had been friends, Liz admitted: "I didn't want John to have anything to do with him, but he did. Levy was around John's age. He might have been one of Lucinda's kids; he helped John sometimes. He worked at the stables and sometimes at the mill." She added that the Ailstock's were terrible snobs. They owned some land around town and thought they were better than anyone else, but they were alone in that opinion. Lucinda had been her sister-in-law, and Liz made no effort to hide her dislike for the woman. Evidently Lucinda had always looked down her nose at Liz because of her Indian blood.

Becky identified "Eliza" immediately as Liz, stating that there were two Elizas in town; the other one was related to the Ailstock family in some way. When Andrew Ailstock was mentioned, she looked puzzled and admitted it was John's name, but, she said: "Everyone always calls him John." When asked who Mary Jane Ailstock was, she again looked puzzled, then said it was her real name, although she was rarely called by it. When she was a little girl, her father started calling her Becky after his mother, Rebeccah. Sometimes when she was showing off or dancing, in amusement he called her "Lady Jane." Charley always called her Becky, as did everyone else in town except John, who occasionally called her

Mary Jane, but usually used a pet name that she could not recall. It was Liz who said John called Becky "Babe." When John was being very serious or when he was angry, he would call her Mary Jane. After John had the fight with Jake Bauer on Main Street and Becky had beaned Jake with the liniment bottle, John had ordered her, very sternly: "Mary Jane, you go home and stay there!"

January 22 was actually two days after Becky's death. She died on January 20, but was buried on the 22nd. The year was not 1867, she insisted, because the war was not over, and there had been no epidemic when she died. These things came later.

*Charles E. Patterson*
*photo courtesy of M.A. West Point*

# CHAPTER TEN

## WEST POINT

EARLY IN THIS STUDY, Charley had described the battle in which he was wounded. In the regression, he was certain that it had been in Tennessee, and the name "Shiloh" was mentioned. When he came out of trance, he asked: "Where is Shiloh?" No one present was certain, particularly not Joe, so we looked it up and Shiloh, of course, was in Tennessee.

When I went to West Point to search for Charley, I knew almost everything about him but his name. When first trying to establish a background for Charley, he gave his name as Morgan, Charley Morgan. Then he looked confused and said he had used another name earlier. The historians at West Point were very accommodating; one of them did remark that I knew a lot about someone whose name I didn't know. I answered: "That's because I have been talking to him for the past year." I tried to ignore her look of astonishment.

Charley was born in Ohio or Indiana, moved south when his father died or left home, went to West Point out of high school and did well there, achieved high grades, and graduated early because of the outbreak of the Civil War. He was commissioned into the Union Army, left soon afterward to join the Confederate Army, was wounded early in the war somewhere in Tennessee, and was then sent, undercover, to Millboro, Virginia, as a spy.

One of the helpful historians in the West Point Archives told me that only three times in the history of the Academy has a class been graduated early. Once in 1943, during World War II; then the June class of 1861 (Charley's class) was graduated a month early, in May of 1861, due to the outbreak of the Civil War, and the June class of 1862 (Custer's class) was graduated in June of 1861, missing an entire year of training.

Charley had stated that his was the first class ever to be graduated early from West Point. That put him in the May class of 1861. The fact that he had served briefly in the Union Army and then resigned to serve in the Confederate Army and some of the other details of his life narrowed the field to three possibilities. There was Charles Campbell, who, unwounded, survived the war and lived to the age of seventy-four. Olin Rice, who graduated very low in the class, came through the war unscathed and died at the age of forty-three in St. Louis, Missouri. Charles Patterson fit the profile of Charley Morgan perfectly.

Through a stroke of good fortune, a book was discovered about the West Point class of 1861, *They Lie Forgotten,* by Mary Elizabeth Sergent (Prior King Press, Middletown, NY, 1986). This warm and intimate book allowed me a detailed glimpse into Charley's life before he went to Millboro and provided some intriguing details of Charley's official record:

> Charles E. Patterson was born in Indiana and appointed from Missouri. His home is given as Arkansas in the records of the Academy at the time he entered. He reported among the first in early June of 1856, and so made friends with Rosser and (John) Pelham early in his career. He was a member of Company D.
>
> Patterson's record would seem to give the lie to the generality that all members of the Company, and all southern and western cadets as well, were low in class standing. He graduated 16th in the class.
>
> Charles went into the 4th Infantry. One month later, in June, 1861, he was dismissed from the service "for tendering his resignation in the face of the enemy" (militarese for resigning from the Union Army to join the Confederacy) and "joined in the rebellion against the United States."

Nothing seems to have been known of him at the end of the war. Beaumont wrote to say that Leroy Napier, class of 1858 and a Confederate veteran, could furnish information. Rives thought he had been killed in western Virginia early in the war. Lyford, of the class of June, 1861, thought he had died in Memphis in 1862. Malbone Watson thought he had been killed at Pittsburgh Landing (another name for Shiloh).

Lyford and Watson were closest. Charles E. Patterson, fighting as lieutenant colonel of the 2nd Arkansas Infantry, Confederate States Army, was wounded at the battle of Shiloh, April 6, 1862. He died of his wounds two days later, at the age of twenty-five.

But Charley didn't die of his wounds; they just put out the word that he had died. This came from the West Point records, and they only knew what the Confederacy told them. Charley told me that even his own mother didn't know he was alive, even she thought he had died at Shiloh. He wasn't allowed to write anybody. He was the perfect man for this assignment. He was unmarried, he wasn't engaged, he had no sweetheart, no ties to anybody, no one to account to, and he was devoted to the Southern cause. He was the perfect person to send there because he just dropped off the face of the earth, which is exactly what they wanted. Incidentally, that is a small mistake in the book, that he was appointed from Missouri. I got his records, and they say he was appointed from Arkansas. In this book there was also a picture of Charles E. Patterson. We had a picture of Charley!!

John Pelham, a famous Civil War figure, was a close friend of Patterson's. Assuming the cadets were seated alphabetically, they probably sat next to each other in every class for five years. When Becky was shown a picture of Pelham, she stated that she didn't know him, but then said: "I know where I have seen that man's picture. Charley had one in his room; he was a very close friend of Charley's!" Shown the picture of Patterson, Becky became emotional, almost crying. She pointed to a prominent vein in his forehead that can be seen clearly in the picture and said that it would stand out when Charley became angry or excited: "I would smooth it; I thought if I rubbed it, it would go away. I would block it off with my finger, but of course when I removed my finger it was still there." The picture touched off a flood of reminiscence. She said: "His eyes were hazel, although sometimes they appeared blue. He was a very good-looking man. His mother and father were separated. His mother lived in Missouri, his father in Arkansas. Charley had lived with his mother, but he sorely missed his father. He used to talk about it a lot, making excuses for why his father was gone, but the impression I got was that his father had just abandoned him, and it bothered him a great deal. He had no contact with his family while he was in Millboro. One of the reasons he drank so much on Guy Fawkes Day, on Thanksgiving, and at Christmas was that he was so painfully aware that he was alone in life. Even though he had us, he was very much aware that he had no family. He lost a lot toward the end of the war. At that point it became an obsession, a personal crusade to rebuild the South and continue the war. He died about four years after the war. The feeling I get—and I have no idea where it comes from because by this time Becky was dead—but I know that after the war he changed a great deal. He refused to give up."

Everyone in this work, when shown his West Point graduation picture, identified Patterson as Charley. The younger girls, Lila and Elizabeth, became excited and angry, exclaiming: "That's the man that beats the horses!"

Charley's legendary mistreatment of his animals begins to be a little more understandable, although still reprehensible, in the light of this new information. He was not by nature a mean or cruel man, but as the war dragged on and he was unable to either use his abilities or get on with a real life of his own, he became bitter and frustrated, taking out these emotions in his horse corral. The drinking didn't help. Also a little research into his West Point training reveals that he was really ill equipped for a life as a horse trainer. According to Mary E. Sergent, West Point cadets in those days started riding lessons in November of their second year. Some of the cadets found horseback riding a difficult subject to master, especially, as Sergent points out, as some of the animals were downright vicious. She describes in the book how one procurement officer actually advertised for mean horses because it was his opinion that a dual purpose would be served—the cadets would break in the horses and the horses would break in the cadets! Many demerits at West Point were handed out for use of profane language in the riding hall, and a great many injuries were sustained, most not serious, in the course of riding and training horses. Sergent describes a humorous incident reported to have occurred about the time Patterson was at West Point. A cadet had been reported for cruel and inhumane treatment of an animal—he had kicked his horse. The offending cadet wrote a note of explanation to the commandant of cadets listing his name and stated the report was correct, that the horse had kicked him first and he had kicked him back—the offense was intentional!

It is important to bear in mind that Charley was living a life diametrically opposed to everything he had geared himself toward. He had spent five years at West Point readying himself to be a soldier and an officer, training that included much more than studying the ways of war. At West Point every cadet was relentlessly instilled with honor, integrity, and religion. They were expected to behave as gentlemen, to be a shining example of their elite training. Charley no doubt would have withstood a Union assault on Millboro with bravery and aplomb, but he was never called on to do so. He never got to wear his uniform; he could never talk to anyone about the heavy responsibility that he carried on his shoulders, or the honor that his mission bestowed on him. The war raged all around him—he could see it in the valley below him—but he never got to be in it. As a spy, he could never form any really close alliances with anyone, and the only woman in his life was married to another man. Even his mother thought him dead, as did most of his West Point classmates.

The image of Charley, the rough, gruff horse trainer, almost automatically makes one picture an older man, but Charley was only in his early twenties. He may have taken on his cover identity a little too well and for too long. To go from an immaculately clean-shaved, well-groomed, disciplined, and idealistic young ca-

det to an unkempt, hard-drinking, brawling horse trainer was quite
a leap. Millboro was a very small town; the saloon was probably
one of the only spots around, other than Rose's whorehouse, where
people gathered, mingled, and talked. Perhaps Charley originally
hung around the bar to see what he could pick up in the way of
useful information. Later the drinking became a way to ease his
pain.

It was several months before I was able to hypnotize Joe and
introduce him to Patterson. Before I put him under I told him only
two things—that he was right about his name, it had been Charles,
and that the man, Charles, had a prominent vein on his forehead.
Joe took my finger and rubbed it over his forehead in the exact spot
where Patterson's vein was. To my amazement, there was a distinct
ridge, a very noticeable indentation on Joe's forehead. He said
military doctors always asked if he had had a skull fracture, but the
recess in his forehead had been there since birth.

The question was raised as to why a West Point graduate,
steeped in self-respect and honor, would have become involved
with another man's wife as Charley did with Becky. Reading
Sergent's book about life at the Point makes it easier to understand.
Charley went into West Point at about age eighteen. The men in
training at that time lived like cloistered monks. Their only real
exposure to women was during their last year or two when they
were allowed to attend occasional "hops," dances that were heavily
chaperoned and ended very early in the evening. Upon leaving
West Point, Charley was busy fighting the war and was constantly
on the move. He reached Millboro as a normal, healthy young man
who had never known romance, was possibly still a virgin, and was
sexually and emotionally naive and vulnerable to the earthy charms
of someone like the vivacious Becky. Under hypnosis he stated
many times that there were no available young women in Millboro.
Add to this the frustration of his inactivity while his classmates
were all out in combat making big names for themselves, and it's
easy to see why he turned to drink and Becky, in that order. The
drink he chose, and Becky, being ignored by John, chose him. Sex
could be a powerful opiate to a young man in Charley's situation.

To the entire world, his family, former friends, and classmates, Charles Patterson was dead. When Charley joined the Confederate Army, he was commissioned a lieutenant colonel in the infantry. His original story, under hypnosis, was that his name was Charley Morgan and he had been a captain in the cavalry when injured. This was part of his cover-up. They did not want his real rank known because he was young for that much rank, and the cavalry was chosen to make it seem that he had more knowledge of horses than he really did. The Confederacy wanted no one to know he was alive, least of all his former West Point friends, some of whom were making illustrious names for themselves in the war. Charley attended West Point one year ahead of George Custer, and his graduating class included John Pelham, Tom Rosser, Emory Upton, and Judson Kilpatrick, to name but a few of the men whose stars shone brightly during and after the Civil War. Anyone familiar with the regular service knows the tight bonds that exist between military men; they keep track of each other as much as possible at all times. The Confederacy knew that if any of Charley's old classmates were aware that he was at Millboro, the logical question would be, why? Sooner or later the information would permeate into Union intelligence because, despite laws to the contrary, there was a good deal of smuggling of messages between friends in the different armies. Charley's identity and location had to be utterly secret. Why? Because the South desperately did not want to call any attention to Millboro. They expected an all-out assault on the town, but it never came; there is no real explanation for why that was. It is impossible to believe that with all the Yankee spies in and out of Millboro, the Union did not know about the quantity of supplies there. When asked, Charley's initial reaction was that it was basically a matter of the inefficiency of the Northern commanders. History has long taken note of the gross inadequacy of some of Lincoln's generals and it would not be the first time in war that crucial information was not acted on. It was also suggested that Millboro was strategically inaccessible, with all the hills surrounding it. A fight might have turned into a logistic nightmare, but as Charley said: "That never stopped the Yankees before." Their manpower numbers were staggering compared to those of the South, and the brass never hesitated to use the men as cannon fodder.

When Joe was taken back into the life of Charley and shown the picture of John Pelham from the West Point book, a look of immediate recognition crossed his face. He said they sat near each other a lot because of their names. When the name Tom Rosser was mentioned, Charley remembered helping him with his studies and described him as "very dark, rawboned, skinny, and big," an excellent description of the man. Asked if he knew anything about the "Great Chains" at West Point, Charley replied: "I want to say they strung it across a harbor, but that's not right." Actually, it was a pretty good answer. The Great Chains are remnants of a large chain that was strung across the Hudson River during the Revolutionary War to keep the British from travelling up the river. The chains are displayed near the parade ground at West Point today, as they were when Charley was there.

At one point, I asked Charley about the possibility of women attending West Point. This brought a loud laugh and he said: "It would not work at all!! Of course the plebes might have fun with it; there would be a lot of jokes!" Charley discussed the problems facing the cadets during his time there: "A lot of problems, big problems." He was very glad to graduate; he worried about it right up until the last minute. If Arkansas had left the Union earlier, he would have had to leave West Point, as he felt he only had a "ticket to stay" as long as Arkansas remained in the Union. Many of his friends were not so lucky and had to leave before graduating.

Graduation was a very emotional time. It broke his heart to see some of the boys leaving before they got to graduate after putting in so much time and effort during their years of tough training. Charley was only in the Union Army for a month before he resigned and went with the South. He said: "I didn't even get time to wash my uniform."

*Liz (Barbara) studies the remains of her Millboro house.*

*Nesting boxes in Liz's old chicken coop*

*Rose's bawdy house*

*Large cleared area in Robin's Nest,*
*possibly where ceremonies were held*

*Original logs
visible under
siding
on Mary's
former house*

*Old spring and smokehouse*

# CHAPTER ELEVEN

# RETURN TO MILLBORO

ONE YEAR AFTER THE EXPEDITION to Millboro with Joe and Maureen, I returned for a second excursion, this time with Barbara Roberts (Liz). On entering the town, Barbara reacted exactly as had Joe and Maureen: "Where are all the buildings?" The images of Civil War Millboro were so strong that even though everyone knew consciously that they would be gone, it was still a shock to see the town as it is today. Placing Barbara into a trance, she directed as we drove slowly through the town. We turned left onto the bridge that spans the railroad tracks, left again, and then at Liz's urging turned right, down a very rough, rutted dirt road. As we drove slowly down the bumpy trail, suddenly she said: "Stop! Back up!" About seventy-five feet back, she pointed to a pile of boards and said: "That was my house."

From the appearance of the debris it looked as though the building had collapsed many years ago. Although we were not aware of it at the time, it was located exactly where she had always said it would be: "At the foot of the old Indian trail," which climbs up over tunnel hill and into the site of Robin's Nest. Walking around the rubble of Liz's old house, she told me how it used to be. She showed me around the back where she had a little "cool box" that she used for keeping things cold in the stream; there was a big stream of water flowing right beside it. She showed me the path that Little Eagle took to come visit her every night, tapping at her back door, spending the night with her, and then leaving early in the morning. We saw a little shed in back of the house. I thought it was a tool shed, but Liz said: "No, I kept chickens; there were five hens and one rooster." Together, we walked up to the shed and, sure enough, there were five neat little wooden boxes along the walls, chicken nests. Liz started naming off the chickens: "There was Bridgie and Henrietta; old Joe was the rooster." Looking across the road from the pile that was her old house, she pointed and said: "That was Mary's house; it was such a beautiful house. That's the same house [looking puzzled], but it looks different. Mary's house was made of logs."

Returning to the car, we drove down the road, turned into the driveway of Mary's old house, and were greeted by a very friendly man who lived there. Asked if the house had ever been made of logs, he replied: "Yes, it was logs when built, but I covered the logs with siding a good many years ago. I inherited the place when my folks died. My grandmother was an Ailstock." This last he volunteered, proudly, on his own. The Ailstock or "Aushlick" name was very prestigious in Millboro in the past and evidently still carries some weight, despite the fact that there are no Ailstocks currently living in Millboro, at least none that we could locate. Suddenly Liz said: "There used to be a spring and smokehouse around in back." The present owner, looking somewhat startled, answered that there still is. Walking to the rear of the house, we entered a tall, slender building which, according to Liz, is exactly as it was in the old days except that the floor had been cemented over. In the days when this was part of Mary's domain, the spring ran through the little house, keeping food cold.

Next we drove out through the main street of town and up the hill in the direction of what we hoped would be Robin's Nest. After about three or four miles the houses along the side of the road became sparse, and soon we saw nothing but thick, heavy woods. Reaching the crest of the mountain, there were large paths leading away from the road in both directions. Walking about two miles up the path to the left, we found an opening into a long, narrow, fairly level area, where we could still see neat rows of some type of grain growing. Obviously this was the land that the Indians cultivated.

Returning to the highway, we headed up the path on the right and found it led directly into several large, squared off clearings that used to be covered with tepees and wickiups. The view from all sides is breathtaking, the air clean and pure, and the entire area beautiful beyond description. This experience was a wrenchingly emotional one for Liz. She was beyond words, and tears streamed down her face the whole time.

On the way back into town, we spotted a rather large, dilapidated old house set back from the road, flanked by several large trees. Stopping the car, Liz studied the place for a few seconds and said: "That's Rose's old place, the old bawdy house." It was the same impression that I had also felt intuitively when I saw the building. We were dying to go in and explore it. I felt that if the ceilings and floors were intact, we could find the bullet hole from the stray shot that killed Ruthie. But there were no trespassing signs all over the place, and the house did look as if it were about to collapse at any moment. We did not enter the house, and one can only speculate if the bullet hole still exists.

Still heading back, almost into town, we stopped and took a rather long hike around tunnel hill, to the rear end of the second of the tunnels that penetrate the mountains outside Millboro. Although the area is quite overgrown, one can still see clearly the spot where the train turnaround used to be.

Approximately two miles out of Millboro in the other direction, in what is now called Millboro Springs, one can easily see the large, flat section along the river where the tent city was erected during the epidemic. The area is just beyond a wide bend in the Cowpasture River. The tent site area and the old road, which runs into a wooden bridge that spans the river, are now all on private property. The newer highway runs a few hundred yards to the east.

The next day, after extensive searching, we located the big white plantation house that so many people in the story have referred to. It was Honey who introduced us to it in her first regression when she was at the party, dancing. She said they all went out there by wagon and it was a long trip. The house is actually nine or ten miles out of town, definitely a long trip by wagon. Honey recalled a lot of soldiers in blue uniforms, Union soldiers. That was before the war broke out, and a lot of Southern boys were in the Union Army at that time. West Virginia and Virginia were still one state, and it was the biggest state in the Union. Then, in 1863, West Virginia seceded and went with the North. That's when it became a separate state. Millboro is only ten or fifteen miles from the West Virginia border. There were many people in Millboro who were on the side of the North, but they kept their sentiments to themselves. Many families where divided when one brother went one way and another brother, the other. This was part of the tragedy of the war that ripped our nation asunder. At the time of the Civil War, this white plantation house was owned by a man who was a Union sympathizer. It's the same house where Ruthie was raised by the older couple and where Sharon lived during the war, assisting the old man.

From the outside, the house looks very much the same as it was described by people in the group, except the white pillars on the front porch are smaller in circumference than the original ones. The young man living in the house now graciously invited us inside. The huge living room in the front that often became the ballroom has been cut up into several smaller rooms. According to Liz, there was a large staircase off to one side of the room that led upstairs; that staircase is no longer there, and the kitchen area has also been totally rearranged.

Outdoors, we walked around to one side of the house and there, just as Sharon described it, was the huge, heavy wooden door that opened into the basement. We went down steep, stone steps into the small, rectangular basement with natural stone ledges encircling the room. The ledges have been cemented in underneath, making them solid benches. Three of the walls looked like cement or stone. The fourth wall was brick; in front of the brick was wooden shelving. In the upper lefthand corner of the wall, several bricks had fallen away, and we could clearly see and touch the old wall, about six inches behind the bricks.

According to Liz and what I am able to mentally see myself, there is an arch-shaped doorway in the middle of the wall behind the bricks. It opens into a much larger room, probably five or six times bigger than the little anteroom now visible. Before the brick wall was erected, there was a thick wooden door in that archway, thick to deaden any sound that might have come from that larger room. Because it was valuable and expensive, the wooden door was removed before the brick wall was installed.

The sounds that the door was meant to deaden were the sounds of the runaway slaves and, later, Union soldiers hiding in the large room, waiting for their chance to escape through the tunnel to freedom. This, according to many in the study, was one of the conduits of the legendary Underground Railroad. In the original large room, they say, there was a false wall covered with the same wooden shelving that is now in front of the brick wall in the little room. The entire wall, shelving and all, used to swing out, exposing the entrance to the tunnel. The part of the tunnel opening into the house through the cellar room was large and braced with timber. It was necessary that the tunnel there be large, as the slaves and soldiers would hide in there whenever anyone unexpected threatened to come into the basement. As the tunnel made it's way to the creek bed, it grew narrower until it became a crawl hole as one approached the water. Access to the tunnel from the creek was between exposed roots of a large creekside tree.

The creek bed is roughly two hundred feet behind the house, and today that part of the tunnel is filled in. The large trees no longer flank the shoreline, and the creek is nearly dry, again appearing that the water may have been diverted. We could plainly see the banks that used to line the old creek bed, which was then about fifteen feet wide and several feet deep, plenty of water in which to float a flat-bottomed boat.

Liz claims that the entrance to the tunnel room was bricked over immediately after Lee surrendered to Grant at Appomattox Courthouse. There was no longer a need for the Underground Railroad, and the North was anxious to protect the brave souls who had risked too much for so long.

# AFTERWORD

A MAN WELL KNOWN IN METAPHYSICAL CIRCLES has criticized this work for two reasons: first, because some of the people involved have discussed the project among themselves and secondly, because several of the subjects were regressed together. He feels, that for these reasons, the study is invalid.

Never, at any time, was it my intention to "prove the theory of reincarnation," per se. Not entirely discounting reincarnation, I tend to lean heavily toward Carl Jung's theories of the collective unconscious and archetypes.

Jung defined archetypes as being innate, inherited, primordial images, which were patterns for the figures of early Greek and Roman mythology and are the basis for most religious icons. He felt they directed our interests, aptitudes, intellect and in general formed the basis for our personality.

Jung's description of archetypes varies slightly from writing to writing, but in his "Two Essays in Analytical Psychology" (Bollingen Series XX, Princeton University Press), he states,

> They are in a sense the deposits of all our ancestral experiences, but they are not the experiences themselves. So at least it seems to us, in the present limited state of our knowledge. I must confess that I have never yet found infallible evidence for the inheritance of memory images, but I do not regard it as positively

precluded that in addition to these collective deposits which contain nothing specifically individual, there may be also inherited memories that are individually determined.

As for direct, lineal inheritance of memory in this work, our closest link so far is that one person, who regressed to an Indian life in Robin's Nest, has a ninety-seven-year-old Indian grandmother, who resides near Richmond, Virginia. Most of the people in the story remain well within their own ethnic group when regressed and in most cases bear a strong physical resemblance today to their Millboro characters. In most cases personality, interests, and values also amazingly correspond between present lives and those of the past.

Aside from the fact that Elsinore and Millboro are situated on or near a body of water—Elsinore on a lake and Millboro on the Cowpasture River—the only obvious common denominator linking the towns is the fact that both are positioned over artesian sulphur water springs.

Millboro Springs for a while had a hotel that catered to the baths but did not exploit the water to the extent that Warm Springs did and still does with their old, large bath houses.

Elsinore in the 1920s and 30s was somewhat renowned as a mineral spa. After World War II this activity dwindled, and during severe flooding in 1980 the city severed the last lines delivering sulphur water to private subscribers. All that remains today are one or two resort motels offering sulphur baths from private wells.

As far as discussing the project among themselves, this was impossible to control. In one instance there was a father, mother, and son all involved—of course they discussed what we were doing! In most cases it was this discussion that made others realize that they too figured in the story. In the case of Robin (Warm Sun), she had heard a lecture on the story that struck a familiar note with her. She had not known one person in the study and had discussed it with no one. Realize also that it is impossible to convince most people to agree to be hypnotized unless they have some idea of why it is necessary.

The overriding factor of the group discussing the study among themselves is that it appears to have had no influence whatsoever on their stories! In Millie's case (Honey), we were certain that she was a relative of Liz's, but it was not so. In Diana's case (Elizabeth), we were totally shocked to discover she was one of Becky's children. Diana had not read the stories that were printed in a local newspaper and had only a cursory discussion of the subject matter with Jan (Lila). Diana was, consciously, totally unaware that Becky had a daughter named Elizabeth. On the other hand, when Jackie (Ruthie) came to us after only a brief discussion with Maureen (Becky), for some reason we felt strongly that she was another daughter of Becky's, Rachael, but she definitely was not.

Most of the people who took part in this work view their regression to Millboro as a form of catharsis, a vital fragment of their personality of which they were vaguely and unconsciously aware but can now bring more clearly into focus.

Some might charge that the hypnotist in this work led the subjects. This was impossible to do as we never knew beforehand where the subject was going. There exists, among the general public, an idea that a hypnotized subject will say anything the hypnotist wants him to in order to please the hypnotist. In this particular work, nothing was further from the truth.

Conversely, not everyone who decided they were in the story happened to be. Millie's sister-in-law was certain she was there and so was Millie, but both hypnotists involved worked with her extensively, to no avail. She absolutely did not regress to a past life in Millboro, Virginia, during the Civil War.

From the very beginning, our main interest in this work was the incredible story we were hearing. We had no interest in proving anything, although the story and how it was derived raises some interesting questions regarding the structure of the human mind.

Very early in the project, it was discovered that the story evolved more clearly and in more detail if some of the subjects were regressed together. Each one would pick up on what the other said and elaborate. At times they would argue and fight about what had transpired as each gave his or her own, subjective view of the matter.

As far as cryptomnesia being a factor here, it can be ruled out immediately. All but two of the subjects in the story had never even heard of Millboro, nor had they been to Virginia when the research was started. If there had been any books or movies done on this subject matter, surely some of us would be aware of them. Many of the current residents of Millboro have no idea that the town was such a teeming place during the Civil War. We have in our possession however, photographs of the town taken at that period that plainly exhibit the general store, train depot, boarding house, corral, and other buildings.

In attempting to explain why this large group of people here, today in Lake Elsinore, all regress, en masse, to symbiotic lifetimes in Civil War Millboro, we can only speculate. Perhaps this is where the concept of reincarnation might emerge to shed some light.

Call it archetypal memory or reincarnation—these words are only labels. There is little room for doubt that we all have memories of past lifetimes deep in our minds and that it is the combination of these memories that constitutes the basis for our psyche today.

Marge Rieder
Lake Elsinore, California

## About the Author

MARGE RIEDER has worked in the field of experimental hypnosis for twenty years. She has lectured throughout southern California on Past-Life Regression and conducted classes on Visual Imagery and Self-Hypnosis.

After attending Santa Ana College, she received advanced degrees from Newport University in Hypnosis and Behavior Modification. She is a graduate of the Professional Hypnosis Center in Tustin, California, is registered with the Hypnotists Examining Council, a member of the American Guild of Hypnotherapists, the American Board of Hypnotherapy, and the Association for Past Life Research and Therapies. She has published a number of articles in magazines and professional journals. Currently she is researching a sequel to *Mission to Millboro*.